W9-DAX-465

THE

THIRD

Opposing Viewpoints®

WORLD

Other Books of Related Interest

THE

THIRD

Opposing Viewpoints®

WORLD

Laura K. Egendorf, *Book Editor*

David L. Bender, *Publisher*
Bruno Leone, Executive *Editor*
Bonnie Szumski, *Editorial Director*
David M. Haugen, *Managing Editor*

OPPOSING
VIEWPOINTS®
SERIES

Greenhaven Press, Inc., San Diego, California

Library of Congress Cataloging-in-Publication Data

Third world / Laura K. Egendorf, book editor.
        p.   cm. — (Opposing viewpoints series)
    Includes bibliographical references and index.
    ISBN 0-7377-0354-7 (lib. : alk. paper). —
ISBN 0-7377-0353-9 (pbk. : alk. paper)
    1. Developing countries. I. Egendorf, Laura K., 1973–   .
II. Series: Opposing viewpoints series (Unnumbered)

D883 .T44 2000
909'.0972'4—dc21   99-047189
                                                            CIP

Greenhaven Press, Inc., P.O. Box 289009
San Diego, CA 92198-9009

"Congress shall make
no law...abridging the
freedom of speech, or of
the press."

First Amendment to the U.S. Constitution

The basic foundation of our democracy is the First
Amendment guarantee of freedom of expression. The
Opposing Viewpoints Series is dedicated to the
concept of this basic freedom and the idea that it is
more important to practice it than to enshrine it.

Contents

**Chapter 3: Can Third World Nations Form
   Lasting Democracies?**

**Chapter 4: What Is the First World's Role in the
   Third World?**

Why Consider Opposing Viewpoints?

"The only way in which a human being can make some approach to knowing the whole of a subject is by hearing what can be said about it by persons of every variety of opinion and studying all modes in which it can be looked at by every character of mind. No wise man ever acquired his wisdom in any mode but this."

John Stuart Mill

In our media-intensive culture it is not difficult to find differing opinions. Thousands of newspapers and magazines and dozens of radio and television talk shows resound with differing points of view. The difficulty lies in deciding which opinion to agree with and which "experts" seem the most credible. The more inundated we become with differing opinions and claims, the more essential it is to hone critical reading and thinking skills to evaluate these ideas. Opposing Viewpoints books address this problem directly by presenting stimulating debates that can be used to enhance and teach these skills. The varied opinions contained in each book examine many different aspects of a single issue. While examining these conveniently edited opposing views, readers can develop critical thinking skills such as the ability to compare and contrast authors' credibility, facts, argumentation styles, use of persuasive techniques, and other stylistic tools. In short, the Opposing Viewpoints Series is an ideal way to attain the higher-level thinking and reading skills so essential in a culture of diverse and contradictory opinions.

In addition to providing a tool for critical thinking, Opposing Viewpoints books challenge readers to question their own strongly held opinions and assumptions. Most people form their opinions on the basis of upbringing, peer pressure, and personal, cultural, or professional bias. By reading carefully balanced opposing views, readers must directly confront new ideas as well as the opinions of those with whom they disagree. This is not to simplistically argue that everyone who reads opposing views will—or should—change his or her opinion. Instead, the series enhances readers' understanding of their own views by encouraging confrontation with opposing ideas. Careful examination of others' views can lead to the readers' understanding of the logical inconsistencies in their own opinions, perspective on why they hold an opinion, and the consideration of the possibility that their opinion requires further evaluation.

Evaluating Other Opinions

To ensure that this type of examination occurs, Opposing Viewpoints books present all types of opinions. Prominent spokespeople on different sides of each issue as well as well-known professionals from many disciplines challenge the reader. An additional goal of the series is to provide a forum for other, less known, or even unpopular viewpoints. The opinion of an ordinary person who has had to make the decision to cut off life support from a terminally ill relative, for example, may be just as valuable and provide just as much insight as a medical ethicist's professional opinion. The editors have two additional purposes in including these less known views. One, the editors encourage readers to respect others' opinions—even when not enhanced by professional credibility. It is only by reading or listening to and objectively evaluating others' ideas that one can determine whether they are worthy of consideration. Two, the inclusion of such viewpoints encourages the important critical thinking skill of objectively evaluating an author's credentials and bias. This evaluation will illuminate an author's reasons for taking a particular stance on an issue and will aid in readers' evaluation of the author's ideas.

As series editors of the Opposing Viewpoints Series, it is our hope that these books will give readers a deeper understanding of the issues debated and an appreciation of the complexity of even seemingly simple issues when good and honest people disagree. This awareness is particularly important in a democratic society such as ours in which people enter into public debate to determine the common good.

Those with whom one disagrees should not be regarded as enemies but rather as people whose views deserve careful examination and may shed light on one's own.

Thomas Jefferson once said that "difference of opinion leads to inquiry, and inquiry to truth." Jefferson, a broadly educated man, argued that "if a nation expects to be ignorant and free . . . it expects what never was and never will be." As individuals and as a nation, it is imperative that we consider the opinions of others and examine them with skill and discernment. The Opposing Viewpoints Series is intended to help readers achieve this goal.

David L. Bender & Bruno Leone,
Series Editors

Greenhaven Press anthologies primarily consist of previously published material taken from a variety of sources, including periodicals, books, scholarly journals, newspapers, government documents, and position papers from private and public organizations. These original sources are often edited for length and to ensure their accessibility for a young adult audience. The anthology editors also change the original titles of these works in order to clearly present the main thesis of each viewpoint and to explicitly indicate the opinion presented in the viewpoint. These alterations are made in consideration of both the reading and comprehension levels of a young adult audience. Every effort is made to ensure that Greenhaven Press accurately reflects the original intent of the authors included in this anthology.

Introduction

"In order to have economic growth, poor countries need market economies, private property rights, rule of law and democratic institutions."
—Walter Williams, syndicated columnist

"Development must take the people not as they ought to be but as they are."
—Claude Ake, political economist

The terms "Third World" and "developing nations"—as well as their counterparts "First World" and "developed nations"—do not appear on a map. Although Third World nations are clustered in Africa, Asia, and Latin America, the differences between developed and developing nations are primarily political and economic rather than geographic. High levels of industrialization, freedom of trade and political expression, democratically elected governments, a respect for human rights and political expression, and low rates of population growth and poverty characterize First World nations. On the other hand, Third World governments are often toppled by military coups or led by entrenched dictators. War and famine are prevalent. Malnutrition, unsafe water supplies, widespread prostitution and other unsafe sexual practices, and inadequate hospital facilities vastly increase the incidence of serious health problems such as AIDS, malaria, and tuberculosis. The United States and Angola typify many of the differences between First World and Third World nations. The average American outlives the average Angolan by more than twenty-eight years. The gross domestic product (GDP) per capita in the United States is $30,200 per year, compared to $800 in Angola. The problems facing developing nations have led to a debate about whether those countries should seek solutions that follow the economic and political footprints of developed nations, or whether the First World path to development creates further problems for Third World nations.

A predominant First World view is the belief that development can only occur if Third World governments introduce capitalist reforms. In a study published in the *Cato Journal*, American economics professors Steve H. Hanke and Stephen J.K. Walters conclude that increased economic freedoms—such as private property rights, low tariffs, no price controls, and few state-owned enterprises—result in greater prosperity, improved life expectancy, and more equitable distribution of income. According to Hanke and Walters: "Economic freedom and economic wealth are inextricably linked. All signs point in the same direction: *those who would like people to enjoy greater prosperity must work to assure greater economic liberty*." [italics in original] Capitalism may take modest forms, as in providing small loans so people can start a business, or it might entail that a developing nation open its markets and engage in global trade. Economics professor Jay Mandle praises the latter option: "Globalization has meant that numerous countries that formerly were considered to be 'third-world nations' have become centers of modern production."

Although increased economic freedom can improve the overall well being of a country, some scholars note that capitalism can only be successful if it is accompanied by democracy. They argue that governments should not only allow their citizens to invest, trade, and own businesses, but should also permit open political debate and elections that are not tainted by bribery or corruption. Robert Dujarric, a research fellow at the Hudson Institute, a public policy organization, maintains: "Economic development . . . requires a state that is both strong and impartial. A strong state is one that maintains law and order, provides basic services, and raises taxes to finance itself. An impartial state practices equality before the law and respects property rights." Achieving such a state is a difficult process. The British weekly *Economist* observes that forty-two sub-Saharan African nations held elections in the 1990s, but only ten elections resulted in new governments. Political science professors Clark D. Neher and Ross Marlay note that many southeast Asian nations are only semidemocratic because Asian culture emphasizes authority over personal liberty. They caution that these Asian democracies "are only as good as their leaders." Neher and Marlay conclude that Asian nations may eventually develop Western-style democracies when the children of the Asian elite begin to demand greater autonomy and freedom of expression.

While these recommendations may seem reasonable to many people who study developed nations, they are not universally lauded. Professor of international affairs Ozay Mehmet claims that Western capitalism is ill suited for developing nations because it destroys local institutions and does not support traditional rural development. According to Mehmet, the development theories proffered by Western economists have created "the slums and urban poverty that are now the dismal realities of many Third World cities." Some analysts argue that Western involvement in Third World nations has long been destructive, maintaining that colonization and decolonization destroyed the traditional social fabric of Africa and exacerbated underdevelopment. Globalization has also met with criticisms, as some economists maintain that it worsens the economic gap between and within nations. Sociology scholars Gary Gereffi and Lynn Hempel note that globalization has perpetuated economic inequality in Latin America and observe that only the businesses and workers with sufficient skills and resources can benefit from an expanding global economy. Third World analysts also critique the ecological impact of Western businesses and Third World companies that emulate those businesses' policies and practices. They condemn these companies for causing significant environmental damage to developing nations through excessive logging, which increases the number of floods and landslides, and mass industrialization, which creates pollution and depletes resources. They contend that developing nations should rely on economic and agricultural practices that protect the environment and reflect a country's indigenous values.

The value of Western democracy, particularly the American version, has also been questioned. Some writers claim, for example, that the United States lacks true political equality because the wealthy have the greatest share of political power. Sociology professor Bogdan Denitch writes: "U.S. society has desperately overdue social agendas that must be met if it is to be a minimally decent society." These agendas include lessening economic inequality and recognizing that democracies must have an advanced welfare state and strong trade unions. Rather than mimic strictly Western versions of democracy, some writers and politicians suggest, Africa and other developing countries should rely on traditional governments. One indigenous model that has been recommended is African villages, which have traditionally been led by clan elders and reach decisions via debate and consensus. Franz Schurmann, a professor emeritus of sociology and history, notes that such traditions may still prove vital: "As Western-style states in Africa have failed to perform all that well, . . . Africans wonder whether some of the better features of traditional chieftainships and the modern state can be combined."

As the debate between advocates of First World and Third World solutions indicates, there is unlikely to be a universally accepted path to economic and political development. However, in some cases, Third World problems may not be as great as they first appear. *Third World: Opposing Viewpoints* considers these and similar questions in the following chapters: What Are the Problems Facing Third World Countries? How Can Third World Development Be Achieved? Can Third World Nations Form Lasting Democracies? What Is the First World's Role in the Third World? In these chapters, the authors debate whether the quality of life in developing countries needs to improve and, if so, how that improvement can be achieved.

CHAPTER 1

What Are the Problems Facing Third World Countries?

Chapter Preface

According to 1998 statistics, over 840 million people in developing countries are chronically undernourished, including 40 percent of the population in sub-Saharan Africa. Malnutrition kills 6.6 million children under the age of five each year.

Many observers believe there is no justification for widespread starvation, arguing that the world's food supply is plentiful. They maintain that a major cause of malnutrition is policies that hinder developing nations from retaining or acquiring vital foods and crops. One organization that is often cited as exacerbating the problem of hunger is the World Bank.

The World Bank is an international organization that raises money to provide loans and other resources to over one hundred developing nations. In an article in *Finance and Development*, a magazine published by the World Bank and the International Monetary Fund, Wendy S. Ayres and Alex F. McCalla examine the policies the World Bank has encouraged developing countries to implement to reduce hunger. According to the authors, who work for the World Bank's Vice Presidency for Environmentally Sustainable Development, Third World nations should seek to increase agricultural productivity and expand free market agricultural trade with First World countries, emphasizing that the improved productivity can reduce hunger and poverty and be "the engine of non-agricultural growth" as well.

However, other analysts and organizations contend these policies in fact worsen hunger and poverty. In an article in *Dollars and Sense*, economist Marc Breslow asserts that liberalization policies in Kenya have led to a decrease in food production by 9 percent per person since 1980, because looser government restrictions on food imports have prompted Kenyans to buy cheaper foreign foods rather than invest in domestic production. In addition, Deborah Toler, a senior research analyst for the Institute for Food and Development Policy, claims that World Bank policies have led Third World communities to emphasize export crops at the expense of feeding their own people. Toler cites as an example the village of Tandianabougou in Mali, which suffers from severe malnutrition: "To earn much needed cash for school fees and household necessities . . . the villagers grew French green beans for export, which they themselves do not eat."

As the debate over hunger indicates, poverty and health problems plague the Third World. In the following chapter, the authors examine some problems common to developing nations.

"Imagine being dirt poor, yet having to meet a demand for more food, more clean water, . . . and so on every year, year after year."

Overpopulation Causes Economic Problems

Roy W. Brown

In the following viewpoint, Roy W. Brown asserts that population growth in developing countries could lead to increased levels of poverty and starvation and thwart further development. He argues that these problems will worsen if developing nations begin to adopt the high-consumption lifestyle of industrialized nations. According to Brown, industrialized nations need to support family planning programs in the Third World and adopt less environmentally destructive habits in order to ensure that overpopulation will not be catastrophic. Brown is the founder of the World Population Foundation, a Netherlands-based organization that helps organizations in developing countries design and manage reproductive health programs.

As you read, consider the following questions:
1. According to Brown, what percentage of future population growth is expected to occur in the poorest countries?
2. How many people could the planet support if a low-impact lifestyle were the norm, as stated by the author?
3. What does Brown think is the most likely scenario for population growth?

Excerpted from "When We 'Hit the Wall': The Lesson Is Likely to Be Painful," by Roy W. Brown, *Free Inquiry*, Spring 1999. Reprinted with the permission of *Free Inquiry*.

I n [an] article in *Science*, John Bongaarts of the Population
Council in New York wrote about the demographic impact of falling fertility rates. Average human fertility has
been falling steadily for the past 30 years, from six or seven
children per woman in the early part of [the twentieth] century to just three or four children per woman today. But that
number is still well above replacement level—so each human
generation is still bigger than the last. As [Russian physicist
and professor] Sergei Kapitsa and others have shown, for
many centuries world population has approximated more
closely hyperbolic growth as opposed to the exponential
growth foreseen by [English economist and sociologist
Thomas] Malthus—in other words, an explosion. From just
1.7 billion in 1900 our population will top 6 billion some-
time in 1999. U.N. projections [from 1998] show population
continuing to rise at least until the middle of the twenty-first
century and possibly beyond, with another 3 billion mouths
to feed within the next two or three generations.

But, as the Worldwatch Institute has pointed out, the
U.N. projections are based purely on current demographic
trends and take no account of the ability of the Earth's resources to sustain humanity in such numbers. Will the outcome be a hard or a soft landing for humanity? Current in-
dications are that, for some of us at least, the landing will be
very hard indeed.

Birthrates in Developing Countries

Ninety percent of future population growth is projected to
occur in the poorest countries and among the societies least
able to cope. The industrialized nations, the "North," have
all experienced the demographic transition from the histor-
ically high birthrate, high death-rate of pre-industrial society, through a second stage of rapid population growth with
high birthrate but increasing life expectancy, to the present
stage with birthrates at or below the replacement level of 2.1
children per woman. For these societies long life is the norm
and populations are relatively stable.

Over the next 50 years Europe will see its population sta-
bilize or decline slightly as individual couples exercise their
choice of having smaller families. Most countries in the de-

veloping world, in contrast, are still at the unsustainable second stage of transition with rapidly growing populations. The challenge for these countries is whether they can reduce their population growth rates fast enough to reach the sun-lit uplands of stability or whether they will fall back into the demographic trap where population growth outstrips the pace of economic development, leading to increasing poverty, sickness, and starvation, increasing maternal and infant mortality, and possibly even to social breakdown. For these societies, what has even more impact than the absolute numbers is the *rate* of population growth, in some countries as high as 3% per year. That may not sound like much, but it means they face a doubling of population in under 25 years. Imagine being dirt poor, yet having to meet a demand for more food, more clean water, more housing, more sanitation, more hospitals, more jobs, and so on every year, year after year. It simply doesn't happen. Some cities in Asia and Latin America have actually seen their slums grow at over 6% a year.

Reducing the national rate of population growth is now recognized by the governments of all developing countries as a key to their future economic development, but for many of them this recognition may have come too late. Life expectancy is already falling in large parts of Africa as a result of the AIDS epidemic, and birthrates may well remain high because individuals have neither the means nor any good reason to limit the number of their children. For countries in the demographic trap the prospects are truly bleak, and for those with populations already in excess of their long-term carrying capacity there may be no way they can avoid an eventual population crash.

The Effects of Consumption

At the global level and in the longer term the outcome will be decided by the impact we collectively make on our environment. We in the rich North have an unprecedented capacity for environmental damage. We each consume as much energy, use as much water, and create as much waste as about 40 people living in sub-Saharan Africa. We often hear the argument that what is ruining the planet is not population growth in the South but our profligate life-styles in

21

the North. Unfortunately that argument breaks down as economic development in the South begins to provide exactly the kind of high-consumption life-style we already enjoy. So our total impact on the planet is a matter of both population numbers *and* the average environmental impact each of us makes.

A Lack of Resources

Many poor countries are already struggling to support their current populations. Rapid population growth is contributing in many countries to increasing degradation of land, water and other natural resources, and making it more difficult for governments to meet the demand for jobs as well as for health care and education.

In sub-Saharan Africa, for example, food production per person has fallen by 16 percent over the past 30 years. By 2025, the number of primary school-age children is projected to double, straining education budgets and facilities. As a result of continuing population growth, by the middle of the next century at least two billion people worldwide will live in countries where water shortages threaten public health and constrain food production and economic development.

Population Action International, *Fact Sheet Number Seven*, 1998.

How many people can Earth support indefinitely? It depends entirely on consumption. If we all shared the low-impact life-style of an African or Indian, Earth could perhaps support 10 billion of us indefinitely. But with a typical North American way of life the figure has been shown to be closer to 2.5 billion—and there are already 6 billion of us on Earth. The late Julian Simon argued that population growth was a good thing; that by any measure you care to choose life has gotten better as our population has grown, and that it will therefore continue to do so. Unfortunately, it isn't possible to draw that conclusion. Quite apart from the fact that there are measures by which life has most assuredly become more difficult, the problem is that the resources of our planet—even the renewable resources—are finite, and some, such as fresh water, cannot be substituted.

The big question is: Will we learn to live within our limits, and what will happen if we don't?

There are some good historical examples of what happens when population growth and consumption outstrip the available resources. Easter Island is one that springs to mind. When the island was first visited by Westerners in the seventeenth century, there was evidence that it had once supported a far higher population and a higher level of civilization than was then in evidence. In fact, it was thought that the island had once been inhabited by a race of supermen. Research has revealed that a once-flourishing society on a green and pleasant island outgrew its resources. Tree cover disappeared, rainfall was reduced, and finally bitter conflict over the diminishing food and water supply led to a population crash to perhaps only 10% of the number the island had once supported. Almost all projections for future world population growth show it stabilizing at some point in the future. While this *may* happen, it is not the most likely scenario. Human population and Earth's resource base form a nonlinear dynamic system. Such systems are typically chaotic and rarely, if ever, achieve stability. A more probable outcome is for world population, like that of Easter Island, to overshoot its level of long-term sustainability and then crash as crucial resources become exhausted and environmental degradation sets in. Only global agreement and collective action on both population and the environment seem likely to avert this outcome.

Steps Must Be Taken

So how will it all end? It's in our hands. We, the inhabitants, consumers, and voters of the rich countries of the North will determine the final outcome—either by our actions, or by our inaction. As a minimum we should urge our governments to honor the commitments they made at the International Conference on Population and Development in Cairo [in 1994] to do more to help fund family planning programs in developing countries—and to start to take more seriously the environmental impact of our collective life-style. If we don't act now, our grandchildren—even if they survive—will never forgive us.

> *"Population growth in the Third World has often gone hand in hand with rapid material advance."*

Overpopulation Does Not Cause Economic Problems

Peter T. Bauer

Population growth does not thwart economic progress, argues Peter T. Bauer in the following viewpoint. Instead, he asserts population increases in less-developed countries such as Taiwan and Malaysia often lead to rapid economic growth. According to Bauer, population growth does not cause unemployment because it increases the number of consumers and producers. Bauer is an emeritus professor of economics at the London School of Economics.

As you read, consider the following questions:
1. According to Bauer, by what factor has population in the Western world increased?
2. In the author's view, what leads to productivity of land?
3. Why do famines and food shortages occur in less-developed countries, according to the author?

Excerpted from "Population Growth: Disaster or Blessing?" by Peter T. Bauer, *Independent Review*, vol. 3, no. 1, pp. 1–75, Summer 1998. Reprinted with the permission of the Independent Institute, Oakland, CA.

There is ample evidence that rapid population growth has certainly not inhibited economic progress either in the West or in the contemporary Third World. The population of the Western world has more than quadrupled since the middle of the eighteenth century, yet real income per head is estimated to have increased at least fivefold. Much of this increase in incomes took place when population was increasing as fast as or even faster than it is currently in most of the less developed world.

Similarly, population growth in the Third World has often gone hand in hand with rapid material advance. In the 1890s, Malaya was a sparsely populated area of hamlets and fishing villages. By the 1930s it had become a country with large cities, active commerce, and extensive plantation and mining operations. The total population rose through natural increase and immigration from about 1.5 million to about 6 million, and the number of Malays from about 1.0 million to about 2.5 million. The much larger population enjoyed much higher material standards and lived longer than the small numbers of the 1890s. Since the Second World War a number of less-developed countries (LDCs) have combined rapid population increase with rapid, even spectacular economic growth for decades on end, including Taiwan, Hong Kong, Malaysia, Kenya, the Ivory Coast, Mexico, Colombia, and Brazil.

Land Does Not Equal Wealth

Conventional views on population growth assume that endowments of land and other natural resources are critical for economic performance. This assumption is refuted by experience in both the distant and the more recent past. Amid abundant land, the American Indians before Columbus were extremely backward while most of Europe, with far less land, was already advanced. Europe in the sixteenth and seventeenth centuries included prosperous Holland, much of it reclaimed from the sea, and Venice, a wealthy world power built on a few mud flats. At present, many millions of poor people in the Third World live amid ample cultivable land. Indeed, in much of Southeast Asia, Central Africa, and interior of Latin America, land is a free good. Conversely, land is now very expensive in both Hong Kong and Singapore, probably the most densely populated countries in the world, originally with very poor land. For example, Hong Kong in the 1840s consisted largely of eroded hillsides, and much of Singapore in the nineteenth century was empty marsh. Both places are now highly industrialized and prosperous. The experience of other countries, both in the East and in the West, teaches the same lesson. Poor countries differ in density. For example, India's population density is some 750 people per square mile whereas Zaire's density is approximately 40 people per square mile. And prosperous countries differ in density. Japan's density is some 850 people per square mile whereas U.S. density is approximately 70 people per square mile. All these instances suggest the obvious: the importance of people's economic qualities and the policies of governments.

It is pertinent also that in both prosperous and poor countries the productivity of the soil owes very little to the "original and indestructible powers of the soil," that is, to land as a factor in totally inelastic supply. The productivity of land results largely from human activity: labor, investment, science, and technology.

The wide differences in economic performance and prosperity between individuals and groups in the same country, with access to the same natural resources, also make clear that the availability of natural resources cannot be critical to economic achievement. Such differences have been, and still are, conspicuous the world over. Salient examples of group differences in the same country include those among Chinese, Indians, and Malays in Malaysia; Chinese and others elsewhere in southeast Asia; Parsees, Jains, Marwaris, and others in India; Greeks and Turks in Cyprus; Asians and Africans in East and Central Africa; Ibo and others in Nigeria; and Chinese, Lebanese, and West Indians in the Caribbean. The experience of Huguenots, Jews, and Nonconformists* in the West also makes clear that natural resources

---

*Huguenots were sixteenth-century French Protestants. Nonconformists are people who refuse to conform to the doctrine of an established church. The term usually refers to Protestant dissenters from the Church of England.

are not critical for economic achievement. For long periods, these prosperous groups were not allowed to own land or had their access to it severely restricted.

Mineral resources have often yielded substantial windfalls to those who discovered or developed them or expropriated their owners. Latin American gold and silver in the sixteenth century and the riches of contemporary oil-producing states illustrate the prosperity conferred by natural resources. But the precious metals of the Americas did not promote economic progress in pre-Columbian America, nor did their capture ensure substantial development in Spain. The oil reserves of the Middle East and elsewhere were worthless until discovered and developed by Westerners, and it remains a matter of conjecture whether they will lead to sustained economic advance in the producing countries.

Population growth as such can induce changes in economic behavior favorable to capital formation. The parents of enlarged families may work harder and save more in order to provide for the future of their families. In LDCs as in the West, poor people save and invest. They can sacrifice leisure for work or transfer their labor and land to more productive use, perhaps by switching from subsistence production to cash crops. Poor and illiterate traders have often accumulated capital by working harder and opening up local markets.

Famine and Unemployment

Despite the repeated warnings of doomsayers, there is no danger that population growth will cause a shortage of land and hence malnutrition or starvation. Contemporary famines and food shortages occur mostly in sparsely populated subsistence economies such as Ethiopia, the Sahel, Tanzania, Uganda, and Zaire. In these countries, land is abundant and, in places, even a free good. Recurrent food shortages or famines in these and other LDCs reflect features of subsistence and near-subsistence economies such as nomadic style of life, shifting cultivation, and inadequate communications and storage facilities. Those conditions are exacerbated by lack of public security, official restrictions on the activities of traders, restrictions on the movement of food, and restrictions on imports of both consumer goods and farm supplies.

Unproductive forms of land tenure such as tribal systems of land rights can also bring about shortages. No famines are reported in such densely populated regions of the less developed world as Taiwan, Hong Kong, Singapore, western Malaysia, and the cash-crop-producing areas of West Africa. Indeed, where a greater density of population in sparsely populated countries brings about improved transport facilities and greater public security, it promotes emergence from subsistence production.

Faith in Human Ingenuity

In my own profession of journalism it is common enough to deride economists as practitioners of the "dismal science." Yet in most cases it is the economists who have maintained faith in human ingenuity and initiative and who have rejected counsels of despair and control. The majority of them have never been found on the front lines of the movement for population control. And the reason is that the best economists spend their lives emphasizing that economic life is not about numbers, but about the triumph of the human mind when given the freedom to innovate and respond. It is the market economist who argues for hope, who points to creativity when others push for control, who recognizes that people are good, in a fundamental, real sense: assets, not liabilities.

William McGurn, *First Things*, December 1996.

Nor should population growth lead to unemployment. A large population means more consumers as well as more producers. The large increase of population in the West over the last two centuries has not brought about persistent unemployment. Substantial unemployment emerged when population growth had become much slower in the twentieth century. And when, in the 1930s, an early decline of population was widely envisaged, that development was generally thought to portend more unemployment because it would reduce the mobility and adaptability of the labor force and diminish the incentive to invest.

The experience of the contemporary less developed world confirms that rapid increase of population does not result in unemployment and also that the issue cannot be discussed simply on the basis of numbers and physical resources. Until recently, population grew very rapidly in densely populated Hong Kong and Singapore without resulting in unemployment. Singapore has far less land per head than neighboring Malaysia, yet many people move from Malaysia to Singapore in search of employment and higher wages, both as short-term and long-term migrants and as permanent settlers.

The idea that population growth results in unemployment implies that labor cannot be substituted for land or capital in particular activities and also that resources cannot be moved from less labor-intensive to more labor-intensive activities. The idea implies that the elasticity of substitution between labor and other resources is zero in both production and consumption. But the development of more intensive forms of agriculture in many LDCs, including the development of double and treble cropping, refutes such notions, as do frequent changes in patterns of consumption. . . .

Pressure Is Unnecessary

It is unlikely that Third World population growth will jeopardize the well-being of families and societies. But if their well-being were for any reason to be seriously impaired by population growth, reproductive behavior would change without official pressure. There is, therefore, no reason to force people to have fewer children than they would like.

> "While supposed experts attribute world poverty to the exploitative capitalistic machine, . . . Third-World poverty actually results from the lack of free markets."

Restrictions on Production and Consumption Harm the Third World

Frederick Regnery and Walter Block

In the following viewpoint, Frederick Regnery and Walter Block contend that the centrally planned economies prevalent in Third World countries restrict production and consumption, leading to poverty and underdevelopment. According to the authors, the free-market system would alleviate these economic problems. They assert that arguments against the free market lack an understanding of basic economic principles. Block is the economics department chair at the University of Central Arkansas in Conway and the author or editor of several economics books. Regnery is a former student of Block's.

As you read, consider the following questions:
1. Why is trade beneficial, according to the authors?
2. In Regnery and Block's view, how do dictators stay in power?
3. Why do the authors believe that labor exploitation is a fallacy?

Excerpted from "Capitalism: Friend or Foe?" by Frederick Regnery and Walter Block, *Chalcedon Report*, September 1997. Reprinted with the permission of the *Chalcedon Report* (PO Box 158, Vallecito, CA 95251).

"The evil machine of capitalism." Numerous sociologists, leftist liberals, and social ethicists give detailed, convincing explanations on how the evils of free enterprise are responsible for the majority of our national and international problems. They describe how profit is the driving engine of the corporate machine and claim that the self-interested businessman will stop at nothing to attain profit maximization. He will keep wages down, exploit workers, and take advantage of Third-World resources all in the name of profit and greed. Unfortunately, social ethicists fail to reconcile self-interest and greed with the common good.

The Beauty of Free Markets

At last, the beauty of a free-market economy: Can there be a more perfect system that harnesses individual greed and selfishness, and puts them to work for the common good? Socialists fail to realize that were it not for free markets, many of our national and international problems would be accentuated rather than contained. These same liberals and sociologists point to Third-World conditions to exemplify capitalism's course of destruction. They cite foreign investment, trading, and multinational corporations as tools that entrepreneurs use to exploit less developed economies. However, a common-sense analysis of this system and the mechanisms behind it show that the "invisible hand"* of greed and profit actually supports the common interest.

An economic analysis searching for the root causes of poverty and economic underdevelopment in Third-World countries points not to foreign investment, or trade with First-World capitalistic nations, but to outmoded policies of the Third World itself. While, with some exceptions, the United States rewards innovation, creativity, and efficiency with profit, many Third-World countries are collapsing under a centrally planned economy. Instead of allowing Adam Smith's "invisible hand" to dictate people's needs and wants through supply, demand and consumer purchasing power,

---

*The "invisible hand" is Adam Smith's theory that by acting in their own best interests when making economic decisions, individuals are likely to improve society as a whole.

these economies entrust their needs to a single dictator or panel of experts.

Many critics of corporate policy, particularly in the U.S., center on trade with underdeveloped nations. They feel that since the U.S. is economically powerful, any trade is inherently unequal and exploitative. But if these trades did not benefit both parties, they would not be made. In economic terms, any trade is mutually beneficial in ex-ante sense. These critics unwittingly insult Third-World countries by seeing them as incapable of recognizing a bad deal. If the trade did not benefit them, they would not make it. More importantly, trade is a necessary instrument for increasing people's standard of living. Envision a world void of trade. We would all need to be self-sufficient, with each person producing everything he needed. Obviously, this is economic lunacy—all people do not and cannot know how to do all things. Trade allows for division of labor and specialization, encouraging countries to allocate their resources to produce goods they have a comparative advantage in. This explains why so called cash-cropping is an economic benefit rather than a tragedy for many underdeveloped nations. When describing the causes of malnourishment, sociologist [Walter Rodney] said that "because of government incentives and foreign pressure, Brazil is abandoning traditional crops such as potatoes and black beans, for more exotic, export-orientated crops." He obviously fails to comprehend the basic concept of comparative advantage. By producing the crops they are most efficient at farming and then trading for staples, they end up with more food than had they stuck to traditional foods. The Brazilians are not as stupid or easily manipulated as one might think.

Multinational Corporations Are Helpful

Apparently, any economic foreign relations are manipulative and unfair. The "humanitarians" are quick to criticize foreign investment, and multinational corporations in particular. In their view, these corporations overwhelm and exploit their economy and politics by underpaying workers to produce products the country does not need. In the words of an eminent social ethicist [Penney Lernoux], the political costs of foreign aid and investment may be higher than the economic benefits they bring. Indeed, many of the arguments for corporate investment, while reasonable in theory, do not apply in a region like Latin America, where the governments have neither the will nor the means to control or guide a transnational empire. . . .

Her argument is counterproductive. Common sense dictates that the "invisible hand" provides for the common interest much better than a dictatorship. With supply and demand dictating resource distribution in a free market, dictators would no longer have the opportunity to make irresponsible economic decisions. Government intervention cannot compete with the checks and balances inherent in a market economy. A dictator stays in power by killing competition, which leads to inefficiency, increasing prices, and underdevelopment. On the other hand, multinational corporations stay in power by beating competition, and this results in increased efficiency, lower prices, and greater consumer choice. Profit maximization leads to consumer satisfaction. Multinationals should be a welcome alternative to a dictatorship's counterproductive motives. Yet another economic fallacy promoted by Lernoux and other "ethicists" concerns the types of industry promoted by multinationals as counterproductive to economic development:

> Do you make refrigerators and air conditioners or shirts and shoes? Do you build sophisticated hospitals or rural clinics? By choosing to encourage foreign investment in such tech-

Barriers to Production

The sad fact is that in . . . poor countries like Burundi, indigenous political and cultural barriers to production constitute the overwhelming if not exclusive source of poverty. Routinely, the chronically destitute nations of the world are the ones that make war on private property, keep out foreign investment, impose viciously punitive taxes and regulations, spend inordinate sums on the military, squander resources on corruption and public works boondoggles, and in general, penalize or even kill anybody with enough spunk to start a business. These nations don't consume much because, as a result of these barriers, they don't produce much.

Lawrence W. Reed, *Freeman*, January 1999.

nologically sophisticated industries as television sets or computers, a Latin American country may actually be postponing any real hope of development.

This confused logic, when implemented, only stunts economic growth. Any profits these corporations realize from cheaper production costs will be passed along. For example, production costs are cheaper for televisions in Latin America than in the U.S. If produced there, prices will fall, output will expand, and profits will increase. With U.S. citizens now paying less for a television, they will have more disposable income to spend on foreign goods. This increase in demand for foreign goods expands output in Latin America. This increased output means an increase in jobs. With more companies competing for labor, wages and the standard of living will rise. Although Latin Americans may have not needed televisions, they reap the benefits of the increased efficiency.

Basic Economic Principles

Finally, does labor exploitation occur when corporations take advantage of low-wage rates? Critics contend that corporate America constantly applies a downward pressure on wages to achieve profit maximization. Once again, this theory fails to take into account the most basic economic principles. Prevailing wages are determined by the simple laws of supply and demand. A corporation can offer a wage either above, below, or equal to the current wage. If the wage is above, the worker is better off. If it is the same, his situation is unchanged. If the offered wage is below current wages, he will refuse the job, and corporations will have no option but to raise wages in order to entice workers.

In dispelling many of the myths accompanying foreign investment, multinational corporations, and capitalism, economic logic prevails over economically ignorant social ethicist rhetoric. While supposed experts attribute world poverty to the exploitative capitalistic machine, even an economics 101 student can understand that Third-World poverty actually results from the lack of free markets. A dictator or centrally planned economy in no way substitutes for a market economy whose "invisible hand" steers self-interest to the common good. Whereas self-interest and common interest are at odds for a dictator, the two complement each other in capitalism. The argument for foreign investment as exploitation is false. On the contrary, we desperately need a global economy where market forces determine production and consumption.

"It would take nearly 9 billion Indians to do the same amount of environmental damage as the 263 million people who now live in the United States."

Western Levels of Production and Consumption Would Harm the Third World

David Nicholson-Lord

In the following viewpoint, David Nicholson-Lord maintains that the Third World should not mimic Western levels of energy consumption because the impact on the environment would be devastating. He contends that higher rates of population are only problematic if accompanied by a high-consumption lifestyle. According to Nicholson-Lord, the West should consider adopting Third World lifestyles, rather than the other way around. Nicholson-Lord writes for the London newspapers *The Independent* and *The Independent on Sunday.*

As you read, consider the following questions:
1. According to UN statistics cited by Nicholson-Lord, what is the potential world population in 2050?
2. Why has congestion increased at a greater rate than population in the West, in the author's opinion?
3. What is the "myth of Third World guilt," according to the author?

Excerpted from "Population and the UN," by David Nicholson-Lord, *Resurgence*, January/February 1996. Reprinted with the permission of David Nicholson-Lord.

The world's population will continue to grow by at least 86 million a year for the next twenty years, taking global population from 5.7 billion [in 1996] to 7.8 billion by 2015. Thereafter, figures become more speculative, depending partly on the success of family-planning. By 2050, according to the UN, world population could be anything from 7.9 to 11.9 billion.

It is easy to be frightened by such figures and by the acceleration of world population. It took the world until about 1800 to reach its first billion of population, another 123 years, till 1929, to reach its second, and a further thirty-three years for its third. The last three billions have taken fourteen, thirteen and eleven years respectively.

Third World Fertility Has Declined

Yet there has been progress. In the late 1960s only 14% of couples in the Third World used contraceptives. Today that figure is 57%. The fertility rate—again, in the Third World—has declined from 6.1 children per mother in the 1950s to 3.7 today. Much of this has been achieved by an old-fashioned focus on family-planning rather than the broader notions now being espoused. Without such achievements, the world population would now be significantly greater.

Within such totals, the figures that tell the story of rising numbers are the gross demographic indicators—the overall population of a state, the rate at which it is increasing, the total fertility rate. The UK, for instance, has a population of 58.3 million, a projected annual rise of 0.3% over the next five years and a fertility rate—the number of children a woman would expect to have between the ages of fifteen and forty-nine—of 1.8 1. The figures for the United States are 263 million, 0.9% and 2.08.

Compare these with the figures for the Third World and the contrast seems clear. India has a population of 935 million, an annual growth rate of 1.8% and fertility of 3.59. Bangladesh's population is 120 million, its growth rate is 2.2% and fertility is 4.13. Most such indicators cited by the UN are worse, often much worse, for the Third World than The West. There is just one exception—energy consumption.

Consumption and Lifestyles

Energy consumption, however, happens to be one of the best measures of human impact. It describes, for example, how human beings travel—by foot (negligible energy consumption), bicycle (a little more—bikes have to be manufactured, using materials, fuel, transport costs), bus and train (more again) or car (much more).

It also describes their lifestyles. Piped gas mains and electricity require exploration, generation, distribution—which means raw materials, factories, power stations, lorries. Convenience diets mean food factories, warehouses, roads, supermarkets—more energy use. The information economy requires the felling and replanting of forests, their shipment as newsprint, their transformation into newspapers, magazines and junk mail.

Which best fits our idea of environmental damage—the numerical size of a population or the amount of mess it makes? Common sense—and population ecology—supply the same answer. According to the population ecologist Paul Ehrlich, impact is a far truer measure than numbers alone and the impact of a human population is a function of its size, its affluence and its technology.

Yet this is merely a scientific formulation of what we know instinctively to be true. Congestion is an everyday experience in much of the West now—crowded roads, crowded shopping centres, crowded holiday resorts. Yet the population has increased relatively little since those postwar decades when most places seemed empty and unspoilt. What explains this paradox? In the main, increased affluence and technology, and, in particular, the piece of hardware that most encapsulates the affluence and the technology of a modern Western society—the car.

Suppose the West abandoned its affluence and its technology and chose to live like a villager in Bhutan—consuming the equivalent of only fifteen kilograms of oil a year. Think of the power stations and the tower blocks and the motorways that would never be needed. Conversely, imagine the havoc wrought if—or, more probably, when—those Himalayan villagers decide they have had enough of agrarian economy and aspire to the lifestyle of a *Baywatch* or a *Dal-*

las—the American lifestyle, with its big cars and its big fries and its enormous 7,662-kilogram per capita oil consumption a year, 510 times that of the average Bhutani.

This, of course, is the central developmental and environmental issue facing the world today. Population forms a key element in it. But the population issue looks very different when the Ehrlich equation is applied.

One example will suffice—that of India, increasingly demonized as the world's exploding population bomb. Indians consume 235 kilograms of oil each per year—roughly 3% of the typical American's usage. The *effective* population of India, based on American levels of consumption and environmental impact, is thus 3% of 935 million—28 million, or little more than a tenth of the US population. Far from being a population giant, it appears, India is a population pygmy—probably ranking alongside Los Angeles.

Increased Consumption in China

In China . . . a decision was made [in the mid-1980s] to provide much of the population with refrigerators. More than 100 refrigerator factories were built, and the fraction of Beijing households owning a refrigerator rose from roughly 2 percent to 62 percent during 1981–86. Recently, moreover, the Chinese government has decided to encourage greater private car ownership, which now amounts to only one out of 20. Plans are that by the end of [the 1990s], China will be producing 3 million vehicles a year, up from the current 1.3 million, but half of them will be cars, up from one quarter during [1995]. Similarly, a great deal of publicity has recently been given to the consumer aspirations of the Indian middle classes, now said to number in the hundreds of millions. The emerging Chinese middle class, like that of India and the wealthy elites of all underdeveloped countries, is set to follow western middle-class consumption patterns as closely as possible.

Dorothy Stein, *Contention*, Winter 1996.

You can do the calculation in reverse, too. Using Indian figures as a basis for comparison, the effective population of the US is thirty-three times its numerical size of 263 million—that is, 8.7 billion. Expressed another way, it would take nearly 9 billion Indians to do the same amount of environmental damage as the 263 million people who now live in the United States.

The Transition Theory

You will not find such calculations in the UN report, of course. More disturbingly, you will find little evidence of the kind of thinking that underpins them. What you will find, for all the political correctness and talk of empowerment, is our old friend the demographic transition.

The demographic transition is the theory that purports to explain the modern cycles of population growth. Developed in the 1940s by the demographer Frank Notestein, it draws heavily on the European experience of the last two or three centuries, arguing that there are three social stages involved in population dynamics. In the first, typical of "pre-modern" societies, birth and death rates are both high: population growth is slow. In the second, better living conditions bring lower death rates. Births, however, remain the same: population growth is rapid. In the third stage, economic and social gains reduce the desire for big families: birth and death rates are in equilibrium and growth levels off.

There are several possible objections to the theory, not the least of which is that it is a rationalization, and also a universalization, of European history. In the wrong hands, the demographic transition can instil an overwhelming, but largely misplaced, faith in Western-style development as the cure for population growth.

The UN's thinking on population control exudes such a faith—a faith, in effect, in both the inevitability and the desirability of urbanization and industrialization. Here are a few samples from the United Nations Population Fund's (UNFPA's) report:

". . . the process of migration, including urbanization, is an intrinsic aspect of development which brings many benefits to both the migrants themselves and society in general . . ."

"The decades ahead are destined to produce a further shift of rural populations to urban areas as well as continued high levels of migration between countries. These migrations are an important part of the economic transformations occurring around the globe."

"The economic advancement of women is integrally related to population growth, sustainable development and economic advancement. There is a strong correspondence between countries where women have advanced and those where economic growth has been steady, and between those where women's participation is hindered and those where there has been stagnation."

People Are Not the Problem

Such thinking compounds the myth of Third World guilt. It says that not only are less developed countries producing more human beings: the reason they are doing so lies in their lack of (Western-style) development. The possibility of leapfrogging urbanism, the cash economy and industrialization into a wholly different type of society—decentralized, smaller-scale, rural, community-based—hardly enters into the calculations, even though this is the model the West itself now seems to be groping towards. Yet perhaps the most alarming feature is the insidious hold which such ideas appear to exercise on the minds of UN officials, operating at a scarcely conscious level, as though they were a set of self-evident assumptions like the roundness of the Earth or the laws of gravity.

The truth is that more people are not in themselves a bad thing: it depends how they live. More Americans are bad news, more Bhutanis possibly not. Nor is economic wealth an automatic cure-all. Initially it is a great destroyer of environments. We know this not only from history—the vanished temperate forests, for instance—but also from contemporary illustration—our extravagant Western lifestyles, to take one example. At some point in the future, we in the West may clean up our act and reduce our planetary impact to the levels of countries like Bhutan. For the moment, for all our wealth and much-vaunted population stability, we are much the greater polluters.

5

> "In general, women experience neither the reproductive or sexual health they have a right to enjoy."

Women in the Third World Lack Sexual Freedom

Deborah L. Billings

Women in Southern, or Third World, nations face a variety of health problems because they do not have sexual freedom, Deborah L. Billings contends in the following viewpoint. According to Billings, these problems include maternal mortality, sexually transmitted diseases, and violence against women, and occur at much higher rates than in the industrialized Northern nations. She argues that women's health is a human rights issue that needs to be addressed by women's organizations and governments. Billings is a research associate for IPAS, a nonprofit organization that works to improve female reproductive health.

As you read, consider the following questions:

1. How many women die each year from pregnancy-related causes, according to the author?
2. According to Billings, why do some cultures practice female genital mutilation?
3. Why does Billings believe women's health issues should be viewed from the human rights perspective?

Excerpted from "Sexual and Reproductive Rights: Woman-Centered, Activist Agendas," by Deborah L. Billings, *Against the Current*, July/August 1997. Reprinted with the permission of *Against the Current*.

Both sexual and reproductive rights entail a woman's rights to her bodily integrity and control, freedom from sexual violence, coercive medical practices including forced abortion, forced pregnancy and childbearing, and unsafe contraceptive methods. This also implies that health care providers must trust and take seriously women's decisions regarding their bodies, a response which is currently all too rare. Examples abound, for example, in the Dominican Republic, Egypt, Indonesia, and Thailand, where women's requests to have their Norplant contraceptive implants removed were denied despite their concerns about irregular bleeding, a sign for many women of ill-health.

The Status of Women's Health

Activists, policy makers, and health care providers who truly care about health within a rights framework face numerous challenges as they work to improve the overall health status of girls and women throughout the world. The summary paragraphs below outline some of the main reproductive and sexual health issues which need to be addressed from within a rights framework if women are to participate more fully in social life.

Pregnancy-Related Mortality and Morbidity: Around the world, 585,000 women die annually from pregnancy-related causes, most commonly hemorrhage, infection, unsafe abortion, hypertensive disorders, and obstructed labor. Approximately 15 million more women suffer from pregnancy-related injuries and infections which often go untreated and may be debilitating and lifelong. Ninety-nine percent of all pregnancy-related deaths occur in Southern countries, a full forty percent in African countries alone.

Unsafe Abortion: Unsafe abortion is defined by the World Health Organization (WHO) as "a procedure for terminating unwanted pregnancy either by persons lacking the necessary skills or in an environment lacking minimal medical standards or both." In most countries throughout the world, legislation regulating induced abortion is either very or rather strict, allowing it only under narrowly defined circumstances such as rape, incest, or a threat to the woman's physical or mental health. Over 20 million women undergo unsafe abortions each year, and the WHO estimates that 75,000 to 80,000 of these women die as a result. Millions more suffer from complications often leading to permanent conditions including infertility and chronic pain. Notably, the incidence of death and severe morbidity is highest in those countries where abortion legislation is most restrictive.

Women's risk of death from unsafe abortion varies greatly between North and South, highlighting the differential access that women have to safe, legal abortion services and adequate health care services in case of complications. In Africa, one in every 150 women who experience an unsafe abortion risks dying while only 1 in 3,700 women in Northern countries runs this risk. An estimated 50 million other women in Southern countries suffer short and long-term complications related to unsafe abortion, including infection, infertility and chronic pain.

Sexually Transmitted Diseases (STDs), Reproductive Tract Infections (RTIs), and HIV/AIDS: AIDS is now one of the leading causes of death for women of reproductive age throughout the world as heterosexual transmission is the fastest growing mechanism of infection. In 1994 alone, 500,000 women died from AIDS. By the year 2000 an estimated 13 million women will be infected with HIV, for the first time equaling the number of men projected to be infected.

Recent studies based in Africa, Latin America, and Asia report that RTIs—including STDs, and infection due to poorly performed gynecological services, childbirth, and abortion—are major causes of infertility in women. Sexual practices which focus on male satisfaction can also contribute to the transmission of STDs and HIV in already high prevalence areas of the world. One striking example is the practice of 'dry sex' in areas of southern Africa where women apply drying agents to their vagina in order to enhance their male partner's sensation. During sexual intercourse, lesions are likely to open thereby facilitating transmission.

Overall, STDs are much more easily transmitted from men to women and the consequences are more severe and long-term, including chronic pain, infertility, cervical cancer, and ectopic pregnancy. Symptoms are also less noticeable in women than in men resulting in delayed diagnosis and treatment. STDs, RTIs, and HIV can profoundly affect the lives of children whom women bear and care for. Han'a's story illustrates this point:

> Han'a, a 16-year-old Egyptian woman, has been married for two years and has one daughter who is slow to develop physically and mentally. Han'a tested positive for syphilis and was treated but then reinfected when her husband came home from work in Libya. Han'a knew nothing about STDs, did not realize that her husband could infect her, and also never imagined that her daughter's poor health could be connected to her own.

Fertility and Access to Contraceptives: At least 350 million couples in the world do not have access to modern contraceptives necessary to prevent and delay an unwanted pregnancy. At the same time, women in Southern countries have often been used as the 'testing grounds' for emerging contraceptive technologies. The use of Puerto Rican women to test oral contraceptives is a well documented case in point. To counter this in Peru, for example, feminist organizations have worked with national and international researchers as well as health care providers during the introduction of Norplant and Cyclofem to ensure that women are fully informed of their choices and their rights as research subjects.

Violence and Mutilation

Gender-based Violence: One-fifth to one-half of all women have been beaten by a male partner and studies reveal that 40 to 58 percent of all sexual assaults are perpetrated against girls aged 15 and under. Women who face sexual violence also face a higher risk of contracting STDs and RTIs. These women are, in turn, often beaten or abandoned by their partners and ostracized from their communities. In general, violence against women is a direct obstacle to women's participation in community and extra-community life.

Forced prostitution/sexual slavery, prevalent where "market" systems develop in areas of extreme poverty and/or political and economic upheaval such as Southeast Asia and Eastern Europe, must also be included within this category of gender-based violence. Rape, as well as other forms of violence experienced by women during times of war, have only recently been more publicly aired as some of the most insidious forms of systematized violence against women.

Female Genital Mutilation-FGM: FGM, or female circumcision as it is more commonly known, is in many cultures a practice used to denote the purity and cleanliness of a woman as she passes from adolescence to adulthood. It is deeply entrenched within the cultural belief systems and practices of numerous societies, thereby making its eradication all the more difficult. Over 100 million women in the world today have undergone FGM in its multiple forms, ranging from removal of the clitoral hood to full infibulation (amputation of the clitoris and labia and stitching of the wound to leave a small hole for passage of urine and menstrual blood). An additional 2 million young women undergo the act every year. FGM frequently results in violent pain, shock, infection, hemorrhage, pregnancy loss, complications during childbirth and death.

Female Genital Mutilation

Each year an estimated two million girls suffer the practice of female genital mutilation. Only 12 countries have legislated against the practice.

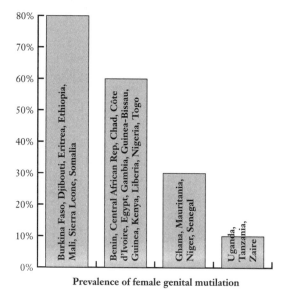

Prevalence of female genital mutilation

The World's Women 1995, United Nations Department of Public Information

46

Organizations, such as the Inter-African Committee on Harmful Traditional Practices, based in Ethiopia with chapters throughout the continent, and RAINBO (Research, Action, & Information Network for Bodily Integrity of Women), based in New York are working to educate the public worldwide about the physical and mental health effects of FGM. This includes working with men, women, and adolescents in communities where FGM is practiced. They are also active in developing strategies to replace FGM as an acceptable rite of passage and sign of purity with other practices which signify a woman's transition to adulthood and which ultimately are more empowering to women.

Cancer: The cancers women suffer are primarily those of the reproductive organs. In Southern countries an estimated 183,000 women die each year from cervical cancer, often directly related to infection from an STD.

While this list of issues may make addressing reproductive health seem a daunting task, women's organizations have taken this challenge head-on. Numerous locally-based non-governmental organizations (NGOs) offer a variety of health and counseling services based on local needs. Internationally-based organizations, such as Marie Stopes International (MSI), also provide services within the local context. MSI is a clinic-based organization offering comprehensive sexual and reproductive health care to women in several countries throughout the world. In Sierra Leone where maternal mortality ratios are among Africa's highest (2,500 per 100,000 births), MSI has offered a variety of services since 1988 including Pap smears, diagnosis and treatment of STDs, prenatal care, contraceptives, menstrual regulation services for unwanted pregnancies, and counseling services for menopausal women. By 1991 MSI clinics throughout Sierra Leone were seeing 4,000 clients per month, mostly low-income women traders in their mid- to late-twenties. MSI provides similar services to women throughout Southern countries where clinics are present.

Women, Empowerment, and Human Rights

Within patriarchal socio-economic systems throughout the world, women have had little to no direct say in decisions regarding marriage, education, and child-bearing, all of which are inextricably tied to their reproductive and sexual health.

Martha Ndlovu, a community health worker in South Africa, illustrates this as she speaks of her sister's experience:

> In the early 1970s, my father forced my elder sister to get married. My sister was fourteen at the time, and she disagreed with him because she felt she was too young. But my father kept insisting and threatened to throw my sister out of the house if she disobeyed him. He went to a man who paid R200 as lobola [bride price] and then let this man come and collect my sister. My father just frittered that money away.
>
> My sister was very unhappy in her marriage, but there was nothing she could do about the situation. She did not love the man, and he kept beating her because they could not live together. My sister became lean and ill. She had a heart attack and had to take constant medication. She has not been allowed to go to school, and she has to look after four children. Generally, married women are not allowed to make any decisions or say anything which contradicts their husbands. They cannot use contraception of any kind because they should "give birth until the babies are finished inside the stomach." It does not matter whether you give birth ten or fourteen times.

While generally having less influence than their male partners in decisions regarding their own reproductive and sexual health, women have had an even smaller voice in the creation of programs and policies which directly affect them. To change this approach, feminist activists who focus on reproductive health and rights insist on reframing the usual question of, "Does program X improve women's health?" to, "What is the nature and extent of women's health problems and what, according to women in their varying life contexts, will be the best ways to address these problems?" This approach entails viewing health as a personal, political, and social experience rather than an exclusively epidemiological phenomenon or a matter of population reduction. Understanding women's needs and preferences in this way must begin with women themselves.

From the preceding discussion of women's contemporary health status worldwide, it is clear that, in general, women experience neither the reproductive or sexual health they have a right to enjoy. Given this, it is imperative that struggles for improving women's health be placed within the framework of human rights, an approach which focuses on empowerment and legitimization. A human rights perspective turns women from objects into subjects of action and policy and legitimizes their concerns and needs as central to programs and policies which they help to develop.

States are also key actors in improving women's health since, ultimately, they are responsible for guaranteeing the exercise of human rights and for preventing their violation. When we frame sexual and reproductive rights, as well as other health rights, as human rights we are then able to tap into international mechanisms for scrutinizing and assessing states' actions toward the fulfillment of these rights. Activists now have at hand a wide array of tools from which to draw in their work to demand that states enforce and implement agreements which they signed.

Raising and politicitizing our demands for human rights, including the sexual and reproductive rights of women internationally, will contribute significantly toward improving women's health and respecting women's rights as human rights. These are basic steps called for in global conferences, including the 1995 Beijing Conference on Women. Ultimately, respect for and active compliance with human rights are necessary if women are to be active and equal participants in the construction of present and future societies.

"Poverty is by far the biggest problem facing women in the third world."

Poverty Is a Greater Concern Than Sexual Freedom to Women in the Third World

Helen Searls

In September 1995, the UN Fourth World Conference on Women convened in Beijing, China, to discuss violence against women, abortion, and related issues. In the following viewpoint, written prior to that conference, Helen Searls asserts that the agenda is misguided and reflects the biases of Western feminists and politicians. According to Searls, women in the Third World are more concerned about poverty than they are about sexual freedom or domestic abuse. Searls writes for *Living Marxism*, a British political magazine.

As you read, consider the following questions:
1. Why do women in the Third World bear large numbers of children, in Searls's view?
2. According to the author, what is the misleading message presented by the United Nations?
3. What does Searls say could solve women's problems in Third World societies?

Excerpted from "A Hidden Agender," by Helen Searls, *Living Marxism*, July/August 1995. Reprinted with the permission of *LM* magazine.

A closer look at [the] agenda for women's rights in the third world reveals a peculiar factor. It has not been determined by ordinary women of the third world demanding a better lot for themselves. Rather it is clear that Western feminists and Western politicians have been the key players in setting the women and development agenda [that was] debated at Beijing. This is most striking when examining the issues that the UN and everyone else in development circles have chosen to highlight.

Poverty Is the Real Problem

The primary preoccupation of women living in third world societies is the struggle to survive in degrading and impoverished conditions. Poverty is the single overriding factor that devastates women's lives in the South. The lack of basic resources means that women have to struggle from dawn to dusk for their families to survive. The lack of agricultural technology means that subsistence farming in which many women work is backbreakingly primitive. The lack of welfare provision means that women look after the weak and the sick in society. It also explains why half a million third world women die due to complications in pregnancy every year. On the other hand, women in many third world societies have little option but to bear a large number of children (and to hope that more of them are boys), since poverty means that people rely upon their children to work and look after them in their old age.

Poverty is by far the biggest problem facing women in the third world. Yet the campaign against poverty is only a tiny part of the new feminist agenda for the third world. It is also the least attractive element for Western feminists. At the New York PrepComm, British nongovernmental organizations (NGO) delegates showed little or no interest in attending the sessions discussing economic policy. In fact at the London reportback meeting, nobody could be found to report back on these PrepComm discussions. In contrast the sessions on reproductive health and violence against women were packed out.

Rather than focusing on the most pressing concerns of women in the third world, it is apparent that Western feminists have projected their own preoccupations on to the campaign. Every major Western NGO is obsessed with the question of domestic violence. A whole section of the draft programme is devoted to the issue of violence against women, given about the same weight as the section on poverty. Many NGOs have diverted substantial funds to southern hemisphere projects that focus on this issue. Womankind Worldwide, for example, boasts in its 1994 report that it has helped finance a hotline for women who suffer domestic abuse in Peru. What this can mean to the millions of impoverished Peruvian women living in shanty towns and villages without access to a telephone is anybody's guess.

Feminist Preoccupations

The same Western feminist preoccupations permeate other NGO projects. The development agency Oxfam, for example, thought it appropriate to help fund a Mexican NGO set up by a Belgian feminist. One of the key activities of the group was to publish a book called *Cuerpo de Mujer—A Woman's Body*—which explores the theme of women's sexuality and relationships. No doubt this is a crucial concern for the women of Islington, but it is difficult to imagine that it is the most pressing priority for the women in the shanty towns around Mexico City.

Western feminists even impose their preoccupations on to women in the refugee camps of Africa. In Tanzania Oxfam has established gender projects among Rwandan refugees, focused on the perennial Western feminist preoccupation of female representation. Rwandan refugees may be desperate, hungry and homeless but at least they can take comfort in the fact that women are represented on the organising committees of the camps. Representation takes up another entire section of the draft programme, superimposing the Emily's List [an organization that raises money for pro-choice female Democrats] concerns of middle class Western women on to the third world. Nor is it surprising to find that concern about the environment and women's representation in the media are substantial issues in the programme. These are the issues that Western feminists know and love.

Question the priorities of Western NGOs, and they will

point to groups of women from the third world who are echoing the demands of their gender-based projects. A more realistic appraisal of matters, however, shows that these women are simply dancing to the West's tune. If you want funding from development agencies today, you have to include a fashionable gender angle to your project. It is unsurprising that those applying for funds have learned to dress up their claims in the new language of gender. The fact that these projects may not be the most pressing areas of concern for women in the third world or the most appropriate areas for development seems unimportant to the Western agencies.

If the emphasis of the Global Platform at Beijing was simply inappropriate, the conference could be dismissed as a waste of time. But unfortunately things are more serious than that.

The message [that was] promoted through the Beijing conference, and all of the UN's work on gender issues, is dangerously misleading. It suggests that the problems facing women in third world societies result primarily from the backward cultural practices of those societies. This narrow focus ignores the way that the exploitative and oppressive world system imposed by the West destroys women's lives. Worse still, the message of Beijing is that, far from the West being a central cause of women's problems in the third world, more intervention by Western agencies could actually provide the solution.

Condescending Attitudes

The theme of combating barbaric cultural practices in third world societies comes up time and again in the NGO discussion around Beijing. Womankind Worldwide, for example, states that it is keen to 'support projects that eradicate suffering caused by harmful traditional practices'. Agencies such as Oxfam have published studies arguing that it is backward cultural and religious practices that keep women down in African, Asian and Latin American societies.

The same anti-third world tone can be found throughout the draft programme. Section D states that 'violence against women derives essentially from cultural patterns, particularly the harmful effects of certain traditional practices'. Section I of the programme condescendingly calls for a human rights education programme for third world nations.

In this discussion, the cultural practices of third world countries are entirely divorced from the social and economic conditions which give rise to them. The degradation of women ceases to be a consequence of living in a degraded and impoverished society, and becomes instead a function of the unsophisticated attitudes of men in the third world. This is a line of argument guaranteed to win warm applause in Western capitals. So long as it is third world culture and traditional practices that are blamed for women's position, the Western governments and money men can use the discussions at Beijing as an indirect form of flattery for their own systems.

Do Not Devalue the Family

The message that the United States should be sending to the world is that family integrity and women's equality are not antithetical ideas. Expanding economic opportunity for women, equal pay for equal work, and other principles of nondiscrimination need not be linked to a devaluation of the roles of wife and mother. Instead, we should promote programs and policies that offer women meaningful alternatives to abortion, poverty, and exploitation.

People in developing nations have seen the moral, spiritual, and physical ravages of the sexual revolution in the West. They are sobered by the feminization of poverty, horrified by the consequences of fatherless families, and appalled by 1.5 million abortions per year in the richest, most powerful nation on earth.

Robert P. Casey and Robert P. George, *National Review*, August 14, 1995.

The Beijing agenda not only mystifies the cause of women's problems by endorsing an anti-third world message. It also discredits the one thing which could do more than anything to alleviate those problems: economic and social development. It is now becoming the accepted wisdom that development itself is one of the major problems facing third world women, as one feminist writer [Rosi Braidotti] spells out:

'It has become increasingly clear in recent years that development, which has been conceived as a Western project to modernise the post-colonial societies, did not bring the improvement in the living conditions of the people in the South. Instead, the development process contributed to the growth of poverty, to an increase in economic and gender inequalities and to the degradation of the environment which further diminishes the means of livelihood of poor people, particularly women'.

These pernicious ideas [were] reflected in the environmental section of the draft programme for Beijing. The feminist rejection of development is a bitter irony. Development is the one thing that could help women in the South. If societies became more technically advanced then women could get a better deal. Without development women will remain the most wretched people in the most impoverished societies. It is legitimate to point out the failure of Western programmes to develop the third world. But if development itself is rejected then poor third world women are condemned to a life of misery for ever. And Western capitalists are offered the perfect alibi for their role in the impoverishment of much of the globe.

| *"Africa today has most of the world's AIDS cases."*

AIDS Is Epidemic in Africa

Keith B. Richburg

In the following viewpoint, Keith B. Richburg asserts that one of the most pressing problems in Africa is the AIDS epidemic. He contends that sexual practices such as prostitution and polygamy facilitate the spread of the AIDS virus. According to Richburg, poverty, ignorance, and inadequate health care facilities make the crisis difficult to solve. Richburg is the author of *Out of America: A Black Man Confronts Africa*, the book from which this viewpoint is taken.

As you read, consider the following questions:
1. What is the main cause of AIDS infection in Africa, according to Richburg?
2. In the author's view, why is polygamy prevalent in Africa?
3. According to the author, why are Africans relatively nonchalant about AIDS?

There are currently about 21.8 million people in the world infected with the HIV virus that causes AIDS, but the pandemic is most prevalent here, in sub-Saharan Africa, where a whopping 13.3 million adults are HIV-positive—over 60 percent of the global total—and that on a continent that holds just 10 percent of the world's population. Whereas AIDS infections in the United States and Western Europe are largely concentrated in the so-called high-risk groups—homosexuals and intravenous drug users—the disease in Africa is found almost exclusively in the heterosexual population, and infected women outnumber infected men by a six-to-five margin. The main cause of infection here is not dirty needles, not blood transfusions, not anal intercourse, but heterosexual vaginal sex. And the impact in Africa is immediately visible; I could see it in entire villages in Uganda, where old people take care of young children because the parents in the middle-age group have died off. And I saw it in some of the major cities, where AIDS has taken the lives of some of the best and brightest of Africa's "yuppies," urban intellectuals, armed forces officers, local entrepreneurs. Whenever I picked up a Kenyan newspaper, or any local paper from Lusaka to Lagos, I was always stunned to see the obituary pages and how many young people, in their late twenties and thirties, were prematurely dead. "After a long illness," the reports always cryptically said, and I knew what that phrase meant.

Prostitution in Africa

One of the obvious reasons the pandemic has spread so far and so fast in Africa is the rampant prostitution and the Africans' free-and-easy attitude toward sex. Sex with prostitutes and sex with neighbors, co-workers, or almost anyone else is almost a way of life, especially in many of Africa's sprawling urban centers. African men come from a recent past where polygamy was the norm, and siring dozens of children was the only way of insuring that at least a few would survive past infancy. So today, monogamy still seems an alien concept. And the same is true for those hardy white expat adventurers who have been on the continent so long that they've "gone native." The runaway sex also means that other kinds of venereal diseases are rife—gonorrhea, syphilis, herpes, warts, all kinds of ailments that might leave open sores on the genitals. Western researchers long ago concluded that the presence of other venereal diseases makes it far easier for the opportunistic AIDS virus to find an entry point and make a home.

Almost everywhere in Africa, prostitution is rampant, from the Florida bar in Nairobi to the disco at the mezzanine floor of the Inter-Continental Hotel in Kinshasa, from the seedy bars of Kigali and Kampala to the lobby of the posh Lagos Sheraton, where girls with long, fake braids wink and smile at newcomers collapsing at the lobby bar for a beer after the treacherous ride in from the airport. It's a breakdown of Africa's more conservative social tradition, these young women from the countryside making their way to the cities to sell their bodies for cash. To get a glimpse of the scope of prostitution in Africa, one need only travel part of the truck route from the Kenyan coast inland, around Lake Victoria, into Uganda, and on into Zaire and central Africa. Along the way are innumerable brothels where the truckers stop for a quick night of sex before hitting the road again. It's no wonder that Africa today has most of the world's AIDS cases.

And not all the prostitutes are women, either. Travel to Mombasa, the tourist town on Kenya's Indian Ocean coast, and you'll find the Kenyan "beach boys," male prostitutes by another name, who make their living having sex with the hordes of European women who make Mombasa their vacation retreat. I could never figure out what these white women must have been thinking, other than trying to live out some "mandingo" fantasy. And I was never sure the poor "beach boys" realized the risk they were taking, since they were just as likely to contract AIDS or other diseases.

Of course the widespread prostitution isn't the only reason AIDS has taken off here. The infection rate has been helped along by African sexual practices, too, like what they call "dry" sex, meaning immediate sex without lubricants, rough and hard sex that cracks the skin and makes sores. . . .

Polygamy, the common practice of men taking more than one wife, is another reason why sexually transmitted diseases spread so rapidly here. I often thought about George, my office assistant, and his own lifestyle, which seemed so strange to me, and how every time I gave him a pay raise, he seemed to take a new wife or girlfriend. Even then, I was never certain that George was all that faithful to the "wives" he did have. My phone was always ringing with various women asking for him, and on pay day, once a month, a steady stream of women would come in with their hands extended for a portion of George's meager earnings.

HIV and AIDS Estimates, Global and Sub-Saharan Africa

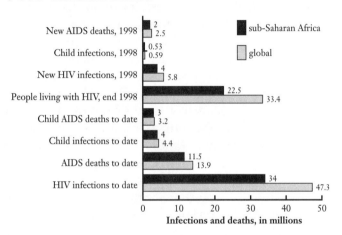

UNAIDS and World Health Organization, *AIDS Epidemic Update: December 1998.*

Part of the reason for the polygamy, I guessed, was that the desperate poverty and the search for employment had separated so many African families. One of the first things that struck me about Nairobi was the imbalance between men and women in the town. Men held many of the jobs that I was accustomed to seeing women hold—waiting tables in restaurants, working as switchboard operators and receptionists, cleaning rooms and making beds in hotels—even my own "secretary," George, and my housekeeper, Hezekiah, were men. In most cases, the men married early while still living in the countryside, then left their family to come to the city for work. Once in town, maybe feeling lonely or perhaps just more affluent, they ended up taking another wife and siring another brood of kids in the urban shantytowns where they lived.

One traditional tribal custom still very much in practice in some rural areas also contributes to AIDS's rapid spread. In some societies, if a man in the village dies prematurely, it is customary for the next eldest brother in line to marry the widow. It was a historic practice meant to keep the widow in the family's protected cocoon and the deceased's property in familiar, meaning patriarchal, hands. The problem arises when traditional practice collides with modern-day reality: If the man has died of AIDS, there's a good chance that he has passed it on to his wife through unprotected sex, and when the surviving brother consummates the new marriage, he is also passing the death sentence on to himself.

Another hindrance to fighting the disease is that many Africans who do think about the AIDS problem tend to become defensive. There's still a large school of thought that AIDS and HIV are a "Western" phenomenon that has been foisted upon unsuspecting Africans. There is a widespread belief in a Great White Western Conspiracy to keep Africans down by unleashing deadly plagues, and more than once I picked up a Kenyan newspaper with some ridiculous commentary or editorial decrying the West over AIDS or claiming—in total disregard of the statistics—that Africans were being unfairly singled out as the largest group of carriers. And when they weren't denying the scope of the problem, many Africans were often out promoting some snake-oil cures that were as dangerous as they were ludicrous if only because they fed into popular myths and the collective denial. In Kenya, for example, the newspapers for a while were filled with stories about a group of young prostitutes who supposedly were "immune" to AIDS. There were also stories about doctors who had allegedly—and wrongly—claimed to have discovered an African "cure" for the disease.

Compounding the ignorance, though, was the problem of sheer poverty. In Kinshasa, I met a physician named Dr. Eugene Nzila, who was in charge of what was once an internationally respected AIDS research center for central Africa.

Nzila also ran his own small walk-in clinic for Zairean prostitutes in a seedy section of the sprawling city close to what would be considered the red light district. Dr. Nzila kept a chart of all the young women patients who came back for repeat visits, and he dutifully recorded the results of their tests. He also sold condoms to the girls for the equivalent of about two cents each. He could have given the condoms away, he said, but he was trying to instill in the Kinshasa prostitutes some sense of responsibility. He believed—reasonably enough, it seemed to me—that if the girls had to pay a token amount for the condoms, they would not view them as a worthless handout but something actually to be used; condoms for free, Nzila said, are condoms easily thrown away.

Sadly, though, when I went with Nzila to visit his clinic, he introduced me to several young hookers in the waiting area who had not been using their condoms—and who were HIV-positive. Nzila was trying to explain to them why they had to come in off the streets, why this invisible disease in their bodies was killing them. But he knew he wouldn't have much luck. These girls would continue to work, and would continue to infect others, because not turning tricks meant not eating, even though they knew they might be passing on a fatal disease to their unsuspecting partners. All Nzila could do was try to convince them that if they did continue to work, then please—for the sake of their customers—use the condoms.

Widespread Health Care Problems

Maybe one of the reasons for the relative nonchalance about AIDS across Africa is that so many other, more immediate, fatal diseases are ravaging the continent as well. Africa is a breeding ground for myriad viruses, germs, plagues, parasites, bacteria, and infections that most people in the West probably never knew existed—or that were thought to have been eradicated long ago. In Kinshasa once, I talked to foreign doctors who told me that they were growing alarmed about a new outbreak of sleeping sickness in some remote villages in the interior. Sleeping sickness! Entire villages just lying down, falling asleep, and dying. I found it amazing that this could still be going on in the 1990s; the reports seemed to be something out of the nineteenth century. More amazing still was that except for a few doctors in Kinshasa getting scattered reports, very little attention was being paid to the problem. In Africa, a few isolated villages falling asleep and dying would rank as a minor health irritant, not a medical crisis.

The greatest killer in Africa, though, is not AIDS or sleeping sickness but malaria. According to the World Health Organization, some 88 million Africans have the disease. (Of the four types of malaria, the most common three are chronic, which means they can recur over decades, while the fourth, which does not recur, can be fatal.) Another 171 million Africans have tuberculosis (TB) in some stage. Malaria, TB, measles, and diarrhea together account for most of the deaths in Africa. Malaria alone kills an estimated 2 million children each year. The World Bank estimates that the cost of lost productivity in Africa because of malaria exceeds Africa's total expenditure on health care. This state of affairs is not surprising, given the dilapidated state of most publicly funded African hospitals, which usually do not even have enough bandages and needles, let alone prescription medicines. It often occurred to me that my yearly bill for dog food and veterinary bills probably exceeded what most African governments spend on health care.

The dismal condition of most African public hospitals is sad testament to the abysmal state of health care. Hospitals, more than anything else, are the main breeding ground of disease and infections. I walked through hospitals in almost every country I visited because I found them a fairly good gauge of how well a government invested in its own people. In almost every place, conditions were, to put it mildly, disgusting. Stiflingly hot, windowless rooms, with flies swarming through fetid air. Patients stacked up almost on top of one another in crowded wards. Blood everywhere. Sick people, most likely with TB, coughing uncontrollably in the open wards. Family members lining the hallways and packing the courtyards, cooking meals for patients inside who might not otherwise eat. If you weren't sick before you went into an African hospital, I always mused, you most certainly would be by the time you emerged. It's no secret, for example, how the Ebola virus briefly flared up as an "epidemic" in Zaire in 1995. There had been Ebola out-breaks before in isolated Zairean villages, but on that one occasion in 1995, an Ebola patient made the mistake of go-ing to a hospital and checking himself in for treatment. Be-cause of unsanitary and unsafe conditions, the lack of rub-ber gloves, and the lack of common sense in dealing with blood, the Ebola quickly spread to the health-care workers, and a new epidemic was born.

One of the main problems afflicting Africa's health-care system is corruption. Most African hospitals are desperately short of medicine. But on the streets outside, any type and variety of medicine is readily for sale, most of it pilfered from the hospital pharmacies or diverted before it even makes it that far. Those with money can afford to buy medicines privately; those without—and that means the vast majority of Africans—simply suffer until they die.

> *"The media misrepresentations that link
> sexuality to AIDS have spawned
> inordinate anxieties and moral panics in
> regions of Africa already afflicted with
> extreme poverty."*

The African AIDS Epidemic Is Misrepresented

Charles L. Geshekter

In the following viewpoint, Charles L. Geshekter contends that Western media and scientists misrepresent the extent and causes of AIDS in Africa. He asserts that African AIDS is caused by socioeconomic problems, not sexual practices. According to Geshekter, the media stereotypes African sexual habits even though African sexual behavior is comparable to the West's. In addition, he argues HIV tests are unreliable and produce a high percentage of false-positive results. Geshekter maintains that socioeconomic problems such as malnutrition and poor sanitation are the likely source of clinical African AIDS symptoms. Geshekter is Professor of African History at California State University at Chico.

As you read, consider the following questions:
1. What is the "heterosexual paradox," as stated by the author?
2. According to Geshekter, how is HIV prevalence determined in Africa?
3. In the author's view, what are the primary threats to African lives?

Excerpted from "Reappraising AIDS in Africa: Under Development and Racial Stereotypes," by Charles L. Geshekter, *Reappraising AIDS*, September/October 1997. Revised by and reprinted with the permission of Charles L. Geshekter.

Whereas AIDS in the industrialized countries almost exclusively confines itself to a tiny percentage of homosexuals, drug injectors, and transfusion patients, AIDS afflicts the same general African population that faces such ancient scourges as malaria, schistosomiasis, and sleeping sickness (trypanosomiasis).

The Heterosexual Paradox

This is known as the "heterosexual paradox" of AIDS. Champions of the HIV model attempt to explain it in two contradictory ways. Some simply declare that the paradox is temporary. They speculate that HIV arrived first in Africa and, in time, AIDS will be just as rampant in the West. However, they've been saying this now for over fifteen years.

Others recognize the permanence of the paradox. They account for it by declaring that Africans are just different from Westerners. They are substantially more promiscuous and more likely to have genital ulcers. How else to explain the widespread distribution of a virus that requires, for nonulcerated genitals, a thousand heterosexual acts? . . .

No continent-wide sex surveys have ever been carried out in Africa. Nevertheless, conventional researchers perpetuate racist stereotypes about insatiable sexual appetites and carnal exotica. They assume that AIDS cases in Africa are driven by a sexual promiscuity similar to what produced—in combination with recreational drugs, sexual stimulants, venereal disease, and over-use of antibiotics—the early epidemic of immunological dysfunction among a small urban sub-culture of gay men in the West.

Media Falsehoods

The research from Africa suggests nothing of the sort. In 1991 researchers from Medicins Sans Frontieres and the Harvard School of Public Health did a survey of sexual behavior in the Moyo district of northwest Uganda. Their findings revealed behavior that was generally not very different from that of the West. On average, women had their first sex at age 17, men at 19. Eighteen per cent of women and 50% of men reported premarital sex; 1.6% of the women and 4.1% of the men had casual sex in the month preceding the study, while 2% of women and 15% of men did so in the preceding year.

The definition of an AIDS case in Africa was established at a World Health Organization meeting that convened in October 1985 in the city of Bangui, capital of the Central African Republic. Under the WHO's "Bangui Definition," tests for HIV antibodies are not required to designate an AIDS case in Africa. An AIDS diagnosis is based instead on clinical symptoms.

For an adult, AIDS is defined by the existence of at least two major clinical symptoms and at least one minor sign. These must be in the absence of other known causes of immunosuppression such as cancer or severe malnutrition. The major signs include: (a) loss of 10% of body weight in 2 months; (b) chronic diarrhea for one month; and (c) prolonged fever for one month (intermittent or constant). The minor signs are: (a) persistent cough for one month; (b) generalized pruritic dermatitis [dry and itching skin]; (c) recurrent herpes zoster [also known as shingles, whose symptoms include painful red blisters, fever, and nausea]; (d) oro-pharyngeal candidiasis [a yeast infection of the mouth]; or (e) chronic progressive and disseminated herpes simplex infection.

Childhood or pediatric AIDS may be diagnosed in an infant or child who presents at least two of the major signs and at least two of the minor signs, in the absence of known cases of immunosuppression such as cancer or severe malnutrition.

The media misrepresentations that link sexuality to AIDS have spawned inordinate anxieties and moral panics in regions of Africa already afflicted with extreme poverty, ravaged by war, and deprived of primary health care delivery systems. The "disaster voyeurism" of tabloid journalism enables them to use AIDS to sell "more newspapers than any other disease in history. It is a sensational disease—with its elements of sex, blood and death it has proved irresistible to editors across the world," [according to James Deane, executive director of the Panos Institute].

Public health nowadays seems to require alarmism and salesmanship, not skepticism. The media's appetite for scary scenarios and its disdain for alternative perspectives enables it to treat Africa in apocalyptic terms. This marketing of anxiety is supposed to promote behavior modification programs to "save Africa." Oblivious to the morbidity and mortality data from the Global Burden of Disease Study, journalists [at the *Economist*] reflexively maintain that "AIDS is by far the most serious threat to life in Africa."

The serious consequences of claiming that millions of Africans are threatened by infectious AIDS makes it politically acceptable to use the continent as a laboratory for vaccine trials and the distribution of toxic drugs of disputed effectiveness like didanosine (ddI) and azidothymidine (AZT). On the other hand, campaigns that advocate monogamy or abstinence and ubiquitous media claims that "safe sex" is the only way to avoid AIDS inadvertently scare Africans from visiting a public health clinic for fear of receiving a "fatal" AIDS diagnosis. Even Africans "with treatable medical conditions (such as tuberculosis) who perceive themselves as having HIV infection fail to seek medical attention because they think that they have an untreatable disease," [writes Dr. Chifumbo Chintu in the *Lancet*].

Some Western scientists, including Dr. Luc Montagnier, the French virologist who first identified HIV, claim that the African practice of female circumcision facilitates the spread of AIDS.

Yet Djibouti, Somalia, Egypt, and Sudan, where female genital mutilation is the most widespread, are among the countries with the lowest incidence of AIDS.

Does the "AIDS epidemic" in Africa portend the future of the developed world? The scientific establishment certainly thinks so. Biomedical funds that had been earmarked to fight African malaria, tuberculosis, and leprosy are now diverted into sex counseling and condom distribution, while social scientists have shifted their attention to behavior modification programs and AIDS awareness surveys.

HIV Tests and Disease

A careful reappraisal of AIDS in Africa must recognize that HIV tests are notoriously unreliable among African populations where antibodies against endemic conventional viruses and microbes cross-react to produce ludicrously high false-positive results. For instance, a 1994 study on central Africa reported that the microbes responsible for tuberculosis and leprosy were so prevalent that over 70% of the HIV-positive test results there were false.

The study also showed that HIV antibody tests register positive in HIV-free people whose immune systems are compromised for a wide variety of reasons, including chronic parasitic infections and anemia brought on by malaria.

The Criteria for AIDS in Africa

On the grounds that the health services of most African countries cannot afford the diagnostic tests for AIDS, the World Health Organisation has different criteria for defining AIDS in Africa, based on signs and symptoms only, from AIDS in the rest of the world. This case definition includes patients who have prolonged cough, fever and weight loss, the classic presenting symptoms and signs of tuberculosis. If the tuberculosis is confirmed but, resources permitting, the patient is found to be HIV positive, it is assumed that tuberculosis has developed because the patient is infected with HIV. It is then quite conceivable, when resources are limited, that treatment will be withheld on the grounds that the patient will die in any case. It is fortunate that at least some African physicians have relied on their clinical judgement rather than the conclusions of Western AIDS researchers. The implications of both clinical criteria and diagnostic tests that fail to distinguish between HIV and treatable diseases common in Africa extend beyond personal and family tragedy. Both are used, separately or together, to estimate the extent of the HIV epidemic in Africa and will lead to exaggeration.

Rosalind Harrison-Chirimuuta, from Andrew Cunningham and Bridie Andrews, eds., *Western Medicine as Contested Knowledge*, 1997.

The very low frequency of vaginal transmission of HIV makes it hard to imagine that heterosexual transmission can be responsible for high rates of HIV prevalence observed in some regions.

So what is responsible?

Perhaps the tests used to determine HIV infection in Africa overstate the prevalence. Some HIV tests detect entities believed to be part of HIV itself, such as certain proteins or genetic sequences. But in Africa HIV prevalence is determined by testing for antibodies, which are components of the host immune system, not the virus. The fact that these tests react with antibodies triggered by ordinary African microbes suggests an explanation for HIV prevalence in Africa that is more plausible than sexual transmission.

Even the association of HIV antibody tests with ordinary infections does not mean that positive results warrant a prognosis of death. Consider an investigation, reported in *The Lancet*, of 9,389 Ugandans with unequivocal HIV antibody test results.

Two years after enrolling in the study, 3% had died, 13% had left the area, and 84% remained. There had been 198 deaths among the seronegative people and 89 deaths in the seropositive ones. Medical assessments made prior to death were available for 64 of the HIV-positive adults. Of these, five (8%) had AIDS as defined by the WHO clinical case symptoms. The self-proclaimed "largest prospective study of its kind in sub-Saharan Africa" had tested nearly 9400 people in Uganda, the so-called epicenter of AIDS in Africa. Yet of the 64 deaths recorded among those who tested positive for HIV antibodies, only *five* were diagnosed as AIDS-induced.

If it is not sexual transmission of HIV, then what causes the widespread appearance of AIDS symptoms throughout Africa? The evidence strongly implicates the ordinary, widespread socio-economic conditions that give rise to AIDS symptoms even among HIV-negative Africans. . . .

Poverty and Health Problems

Primary health care systems in Africa will remain hampered until public health planners systematically gather statistics on morbidity and mortality to accurately show what causes sickness and death in specific African countries. During the past ten years, as the external financing of HIV-based AIDS programs in Africa dramatically increased, money for studying other health problems remained static, even though deaths from malaria, tuberculosis, neo-natal tetanus, respiratory diseases, and diarrhea grew at alarming rates.

While Western health leaders fixate on HIV, 52% of sub-Saharan Africans lack access to safe water, 62% lack proper sanitation, and an estimated 50 million pre-school children suffer from protein-calorie malnutrition.

Poor harvests, rural poverty, migratory labor systems, urban crowding, ecological degradation, social mayhem, the collapse of state structures, and the sadistic violence of civil wars constitute the primary threats to African lives.

When essential services for water, power, and transport break down, public sanitation deteriorates, and the risks of cholera, tuberculosis, dysentery, and respiratory infection increase.

Former WHO Director General Hiroshi Nakajima warned emphatically that "poverty is the world's deadliest disease."

Indeed, the leading causes of immunodeficiency and the best predictors for clinical AIDS symptoms in Africa are impoverished living conditions, economic deprivation, and protein malnutrition, not extraordinary sexual behavior or antibodies against HIV, a virus that has proved difficult or impossible to isolate directly, even from AIDS patients.

The so-called "AIDS epidemic" in Africa has been used to justify the medicalization of sub-Saharan poverty. Thus, Western medical intervention takes the form of vaccine trials, drug testing, and almost evangelistic demands for behavior modification.

AIDS scientists and public health planners should recognize the role of malnutrition, poor sanitation, anemia, and ordinary infections in producing clinical AIDS symptoms in the absence of HIV.

The data strongly suggest that socio-economic development, not sexual restraint, is the key to improving the health of Africans.

Periodical Bibliography

The following articles have been selected to supplement the diverse views presented in this chapter. Addresses are provided for periodicals not indexed in the *Readers' Guide to Periodical Literature*, the *Alternative Press Index*, the *Social Sciences Index*, or the *Index to Legal Periodicals and Books*.

Lawrence K. Altman	"Parts of Africa Showing H.I.V. in 1 in 4 Adults," *New York Times*, June 24, 1998.
David Barsamian	"Vandana Shiva," *Progressive*, September 1997.
Marc Breslow	"Freedom to Farm—and Starve—in Kenya," *Dollars and Sense*, May/June 1999.
Robin Broad and Christina Melhorn Landi	"Whither the North-South Gap?" *Third World Quarterly*, March 1996. Available from Carfax Publishing, PO Box 25, Abingdon, Oxfordshire OX14 3UE, United Kingdom.
Lester R. Brown	"The Numbers Don't Lie: Why Malthus Was Right," *Free Inquiry*, Spring 1999. Available from the Council for Secular Humanism, 1310 Sweet Home Rd., Amherst, NY 14228.
Linda Burnham	"Beijing and Beyond," *CrossRoads*, March 1996.
Robert P. Casey and Robert P. George	"Just Don't Go," *National Review*, August 14, 1995.
David F. Gordon and Howard Wolpe	"The Other Africa: An End to Afro-Pessimism," *World Policy Journal*, Spring 1998.
Issues and Controversies On File	"Global Population Growth," November 22, 1996. Available from Facts On File News Services, 11 Penn Plaza, New York, NY 10001-2006.
Stephanie Joyce	"Growing Pains in South America," *Environmental Health Perspectives*, August 1997. Available from National Institute of Environmental Health Services, PO Box 12233, Research Triangle Park, NC 27709-2233.
Nicholas D. Kristof	"For Third World, Water Is Still a Deadly Drink," *New York Times*, January 9, 1997.
William McGurn	"Population and the Wealth of Nations," *First Things*, December 1996. Available from the Institute on Religion and Public Life, 156 Fifth Ave., Suite 400, New York, NY 10010.
David Rieff	"In Defense of Afro-Pessimism," *World Policy Journal*, Winter 1998/99.
Don Sloan	"Imperialism, Malnutrition and Children," *Political Affairs*, February 1999.

How Can Third World Development Be Achieved?

Chapter Preface

One way to improve the economies of developing nations is through capitalism. Third World capitalism often entails people starting modest businesses that enable them to escape poverty. One of the most famous approaches to small-business capitalism is the Grameen Bank.

The Grameen Bank, which began in 1976 in Bangladesh, started the microcredit movement, a system of providing modest loans to people who lack collateral. The first loans provided by Grameen founder Muhammad Yunis totaled twenty-six dollars for forty-two people. By 1997, 8 million people in forty-three countries, including 4 million people from Bangladesh, were receiving microcredit loans from the Grameen Bank and similar programs.

The Grameen Bank has been lauded for its success at improving the lives of the rural poor and its economic stability. The bank places borrowers into groups of five. If one borrower defaults, the entire group is cut off from their loans. Despite the 16 percent interest rate, 98 percent of the loans are repaid on time. Of the 2 million Grameen borrowers, one-third have worked their way past the poverty line. The Grameen Bank also encourages its borrowers to follow its "Sixteen Decisions," which include keeping families small and not paying dowries upon marriage. According to Ishtiaq Hossain, a professor at the National University of Singapore, the Grameen Bank "is an outstanding institution giving the rural poor an opportunity to climb out of their desperate economic and social conditions."

The praise is not universal, as some critics have argued that the payback rates are misleading. In an article in the *London Free Press*, Lawrence Solomon contends that the system of group loans puts individual borrowers under added pressure to repay their loans, causing them to sell their few assets or visit a local moneylender. In the worst-case scenarios, Solomon argues, borrowers are forced into bonded labor to repay their loans. He also states that the Grameen Bank is able to achieve its seemingly high repayment rate by letting borrowers take out additional loans to cover the default payments, "leading to impossibly high repayments and worse defaults down the road."

As the debate over the Grameen Bank suggests, there is no universal solution on how to achieve Third World development. In the following chapter, the authors consider what steps should be taken to improve the economic status of the world's most impoverished countries.

| "*Countries making the transition from failed command-economy structures . . . will learn from each other.*"

Free-Market Policies Spur Third World Development

Tim Carrington

In the following viewpoint, Tim Carrington asserts that un-derdeveloped countries need to adopt market-oriented eco-nomic policies in order to grow. According to Carrington, these policies include maintaining low inflation and privatiz-ing state assets. He cites countries that have succeeded in improving their economic status, such as Uganda and Korea, and contends that other underdeveloped nations need to learn from these countries' examples and mistakes. However, Carrington acknowledges, a country cannot develop its economy successfully if it is led by a corrupt or incompetent government. Carrington is a former writer and editor for the *Wall Street Journal* and an employee at the World Bank's Economic Development Institute, which offers programs on economic and social development to World Bank clients.

As you read, consider the following questions:
1. Why do some people dislike the term "best practice," according to the author?
2. In Carrington's view, what lessons does Mexico provide?
3. What are some reasons for the former Soviet Union's inability to implement either best or worst economic practices, as cited by the author?

Excerpted from "A New Textbook for Emerging Economies: Learning to Exercise 'Good Enough' Practices," by Tim Carrington, Summer 1997, available at www.worldpaper.com/MMI/caringtn.html. Reprinted with the permission of the Money Matters Institute.

The world has learned two critical lessons about development in the past 50 years: that it happens and that it doesn't happen.

There are today real successes and real failures, and these experiences appropriately are occupying more and more space in the development dialogue.

Learning from Experience

Until relatively recently, discussions were forced to follow a more theoretical turn, since no one was entirely sure what might enable poor, unstable, underdeveloped countries to raise living standards over time. Today, the discussions turn not on what might alleviate poverty and create possibilities for the next generation, but on what has—in Korea, or Chile or Mauritius. The key, of course, is to discern what made the most difference for the successful developers, and to fashion ways these practices can be adapted across cultural and political fault-lines.

Still, experience is becoming both guide and guru in development. It means that countries making the transition from failed command-economy structures or from poverty and stagnation, will learn from each other to a far greater degree than in the past. And it calls for new sorts of development professionals, who are less engineers of change—though these are still needed—than observers and transmitters of usable experience.

The good news is that while foreign aid budgets face relentless downward pressures, the stock of valuable experiences seems to grow more abundant. A group of women in Senegal learn to manage a village grain mill, reaping and reinvesting profits, and improving livelihoods and lives. Malaysia creates average annual export growth of 12.6 percent for more than a decade.

The two situations have little in common, except that in each case, something worked. The phrase many invoke to discuss what has worked and what should work is "best practice." It refers to the optimum strategy in a particular field of endeavor. Some find the phrase irritating. "Who decides what is best?" asks one skeptic. Is it "best" only because it has been lifted outside any particular cultural and political context? And would the "best practice" invariably become something else—something planners might find less "good" once it is adapted to local realities?

"Good Enough" Economic Policies

In a quite different sphere, psychologist D.W. Winicott built a considerable body of thought around the notion of the "good enough mother," the parent who was unlikely to do anything perfectly, but whose instincts and broadly constructive goals would serve her and her child well over time. So maybe it's the "good enough practice" that countries need to embrace.

An official with Malaysia's Institute of Strategic and International Studies described the challenge this way: "We're not in the business of writing cookbooks, we're in the business of creating master chefs." The distinction seems crucial.

Cynthia Agyekum, a small-time, Ghanaian entrepreneur ran a microbusiness designing and sewing accessories like belts, satchels and hairbands from locally woven kente cloth. It was a dreamt-for breakthrough when a Pier 1 Imports Inc. buyer admired the products and ordered 17,000 of them for the US retail chain. Ms. Agyekum found a dormant factory in a ramshackle industrial complex on the edge of Accra. Obtaining credit was nearly impossible, but eventually, she secured a loan from a local bank that had begun a joint venture with the International Finance Corp., the private sector arm of the World Bank.

In a few weeks' time, she arranged to clean out the factory space, locate and repair some used sewing machines and hire a couple of dozen workers off the fishing boats and around the teeming Accra market. When electricity shortages threw her behind schedule, she added a second shift. Even so the order fell short of initial levels, but the Pier 1 buyer remained pleased with what he did receive.

This is how development happens—enterprise by enterprise, and messily. The moniker of "best practice" seems somehow out of place in Cynthia Agyekum's Cessa Ltd., though she is certainly a good-enough mother of enterprise, and a master chef in the steamy kitchen of wealth creation in the developing world. So, with the caveat that best practice isn't about perfection, but about optimum results on the ground, one could find all manner of best practices in how Cynthia Agyekum scaled up a tiny enterprise.

Policies Should Be Broad-Minded

While the "good-enough" concept distinguishes itself from perfectionist models, it does imply a certain wholeness at the conception. The good-enough parent doesn't read the best storybooks but doesn't scrimp on inoculations. The good-enough parent operates instinctively from a systems approach, providing affection, nourishment, security, laundering, entertainment, nursing, transport, and finance. The good-enough development strategy must embrace comparable breadth.

In 1993, when I visited Ghana, which had stuck with market-oriented economic reforms for nearly 10 years and was often cited as a budding success story, there were beginning to be worries that per capita economic growth was slight, and that poverty alleviation was all but nonexistent. Among other changes, prices had been largely freed up, allowing millions of small farmers to improve their lot—in theory. One small farmer, Charle Ayietey, told me the real story.

The government, cutting back on spending, had neglected the maintenance of feeder roads throughout the country. The road connecting his village to the market town of Kasua was a barely navigable roller coaster of gullies and ditches. As a result, trucks that used to come daily to carry farmers and their produce to town, only came once a week. Ayietey had to catch the weekly truck in the afternoon, spend the night in town, sitting beside the road with his tomatoes and cassava and sell them the next day. True, he got better prices for what he grew, but overall, life was harder, and business was, if anything, less productive.

The pursuit of best practice will fail if it leads countries to isolate one element in the matrix at the expense of other equally critical concerns.

Learning from Others' Mistakes

Of course, the blind spots and shortcomings can be useful in the global laboratory of economic experience. Until late

1994, Mexico was held up as a model of reform-minded economic management. Its sweeping privatizations and liberalized trade won plaudits from economists worldwide. But its reliance on short-term, foreign capital flows to support massive trade deficits led to a near-catastrophe, defused by a US$50 billion international rescue package in 1995. Mexico provides a wealth of usable lessons not only in its constructive steps, but in its lethal gaps, and, finally in the last year, in recovering from its wrenching financial crisis.

Emphasizing the benefits of learning from others' mistakes, economists estimate that countries can be set back in their development agenda by as much as ten years if they fall into a debt crisis, or wholesale financial meltdown. There is no shortage of countries which, like Marley's Ghost to Scrooge, can warn others of killer errors in policy and approach.

Liberalization in Africa

The restructuring of many African economies has been gaining momentum. Government intervention in economic activity is on the wane. Administrative price controls are being removed, and agricultural marketing has been widely liberalized. Most countries have made considerable strides in opening their economies to world trade by eliminating multiple exchange rate practices and nontariff barriers and also lowering the degree of tariff protection. In most countries, the process of restructuring and privatizing state enterprises has been under way for some time, though it has proceeded with varying speeds and has enjoyed varying degrees of success. Labor markets are also progressively being liberalized. Fiscal reform is gaining ground: African countries are taking steps to rationalize their tax systems, reduce exemptions, and enhance their administrative efficiency while reorienting expenditures away from wasteful outlays and toward improved public investment and spending on key social services, particularly health care and primary education. On the monetary front, most countries have made progress in establishing market-determined interest rates, eliminating selective credit controls, and introducing indirect instruments of monetary policy, such as reserve requirements and open market operations.

Alassane D. Ouattara, *Finance & Development*, March 1999.

The challenge is adaptation. Uganda and Salvador provide moving examples of how countries can rebuild a future around the notion of not being a slaughterhouse. Forging a path out of the nightmare of civil war and anarchy involves intricate steps of rebuilding civil society, reestablishing humane norms, demobilizing and reintegrating warriors and reestablishing constructive international ties.

But it happens. Uganda, today considered a reform-minded African success, was the continent's nightmare nation fifteen years ago. Near the capital, John Bosco Sekitoleko, taken into the bush as a kadogo, or child soldier, at age eleven, enthusiastically talked of his new, post-war life, at 21, selling tomatoes and learning to read. In Kamgulumira, a few miles from the Nile, warrior-turned-farmer Dick Lubanga told of expanding beyond coffee beans to grow 18 varieties of chilis for export to Asia.

The ex-guerrillas were supported by an internationally backed reintegration program that included some cash payments, metal roofing for a shelter, and transport back to the home village. A Veterans Assistance Board operated from offices in each of Uganda's 38 districts to help demobilized soldiers adjust to civilian life.

But how can the best practices of Uganda or Salvador be made usable in Haiti, where a political stalemate is cementing economic stagnation and where civil violence is rising, or in Bosnia, with its crazy-quilt of vicious-minded ethnic fiefdoms?

East Asia as a Model

Perhaps the most critical question in the development community is the extent to which the high-growth East Asian economies can function as workable, best-practice models for countries that so far, have shown far less success in improving living standards. Cultural, political, and environmental differences lead some to question whether Ghana really can emulate Malaysia, to name two countries with a similar colonial experience, resource base and population size.

However, emulation probably isn't the goal. Once the Asian successes are "unpacked," their components become far more valuable in distant cultural and political contexts.

The high-growth economies maintained low or moderate inflation, encouraged export growth, and invested hugely in primary education. These are critical steps, for any country, without which the prospects of success are sadly limited. The Asian high-growth economies also lowered levels of inequity, closing the gap between rich and poor. This not only made policies more sustainable socially, but kept the growth engine alive, since a higher share of the population had some purchasing power.

One fundamental question to pose is whether countries' institutional capacities are adequate to carry out certain practices thought to be "best" and to change those policies when they turn out to be closer to worst than best. The World Development Report of 1997, *The State in a Changing World*, documents the crucial importance of building and maintaining government institutions. In much of Africa, the authors conclude, "there is a crisis of statehood—a crisis of capability and legitimacy." Many countries, they warn, "are trapped in a vicious cycle of declining state capability and thus, declining credibility in the eyes of their citizens."

Governments Can Help or Hinder

The question of institutional capability hasn't always figured in the more sterile discussions of best practice, but it is fundamental. The best possible practice, put in the hands of the least capable government institution, will disappoint. By contrast, a capable and accountable state institution will seek to improve on even poor or mediocre approaches.

Some African governments are making committed efforts in this direction. Elsewhere, the proliferation of self-help community groups is filling the void by developing for themselves capabilities that may have been lost within the state, through inattention or corruption or both.

In the former Soviet Union, the ability of the state to advance any practice—best or worst—is limited. In Georgia, for example, government officials confided recently that some officeholders actually pay to obtain particular jobs, in expectation of extracting waves of bribes once they're installed. Meanwhile, alongside the high levels of official bribery is one of the world's lowest levels of tax compliance, which in turn translates into poor service, low pay of civil servants, and more bribes. The situation exists, in varying degrees, throughout the former Soviet bloc.

Much of the former Soviet world has undertaken certain reforms—such as freeing up prices through the stroke of a pen, withholding subsidies, and even privatizing state assets. But according to the authors of the World Development Report, "the next stage of the transformation, that dealing with reforms that require decisive and clear administrative action, is now severely hampered by the absence of the mechanisms and of the government personnel and resources necessary to implement those reforms."

Thus, the most critical step in the best-practice cycle—namely taking a strategy that worked in one country and tailoring it to the specific needs of another—is likely to be mired in the wastes of poorly managed, ill-trained corrupt bureaucracies.

Of course, as countries come to understand the costs of declining institutional capacity, there are best practices to observe and adapt in rebuilding a functioning state. The benefit of focusing on best practices—or good enough practices—is that results speak for themselves. In sum, life should get recognizably better.

As they have for Nuestras Senoras del Carmen, a village women's group in the lush mountains of the Dominican Republic that makes a profit from consolidated potato farms. Through these profits, the group has obtained electricity and a new two-room school-house for the village.

Speaking for the women in the group, member Candida Anna Sagatis declared, "We have more freedom; we have knowledge. We are better women, better mothers. We have better husbands, better kids." A best practice in practice.

"The neo-liberal policies now in vogue have yet to yield positive results for workers and the people."

Free-Market Policies Hinder Third World Development

Fred Gaboury

Free-market economic policies are harmful to Third World nations, argues Fred Gaboury in the following viewpoint. He asserts that these policies, which emphasize deregulation and privatization, have led to a greater disparity between the incomes of industrialized and developing countries and a decline in economic growth and trade in the forty-eight least-developed nations. Gaboury maintains that these policies need to be reviewed. Gaboury is the World Federation of Trade Unions' representative to the United Nations. This viewpoint was originally a statement presented to the UN Economic and Social Council on July 28, 1998.

As you read, consider the following questions:
1. According to statistics cited by Gaboury, how many people live on less than two dollars per day?
2. In the author's view, what is the foundation of human development?
3. What do transnational corporations control, according to Gaboury?

Excerpted from "WFTU to the United Nations: Do Your Job," by Fred Gaboury, *People's Weekly World*, November 7, 1998. Reprinted with the permission of *People's Weekly World*.

Trade unions are veterans in the struggle for economic and social development. By their very nature, they are concerned with enhancing the quality of life of their members and the relative success or failure of this effort has an impact far beyond their own numbers.

For this reason the World Federation of Trade Unions, with more than 130 million affiliated members in more than 100 countries, considers it a duty to present its grave concerns of workers around the world about the present, rapidly deteriorating, economic situation and its extremely serious social consequences.

In 1994, the International Labour Organization (ILO) had just released a report in which it said the world was facing the worst employment crisis since the Great Depression of the 1930s, with industrialized nations as well as the developing nations facing "long-term, persistent unemployment."

It was in this context the World Federation of Trade Unions (WFTU) warned, "It is no exaggeration to say that if present trends continue, today's crisis will be tomorrow's disaster." The example of southeast Asia—where scavengers pick over the bones of what once were tigers—is tragic vindication of this warning.

Widespread Financial Problems

What was once "financial turmoil" has become full-blown depression with the loss of more than a trillion dollars in purchasing power and the addition of 30 million people to the ranks of the unemployed.

At the same time, currency devaluation has resulted in the bankruptcy of thousands of businesses throughout the region.

Some might view events in southeast Asia as unique—that specific circumstances gave rise to a crisis that is making itself felt around the world.

We do not share that view, and call your attention to a number of troubling comparisons, all of them from United Nations sources, that indicate the bankruptcy of the neoliberal policies presently being pursued by governments and international lending agencies:

- There has been a slowdown in economic growth in developed countries from an average of 2.8 percent in the 1980s to 1.8 percent in the 1990s.

• Between 1992 and 1996 real weekly wages in the United States dropped to below 1987 levels, while the share of profits in gross value added in the non-financial business sector rose by 3.5 percentage points.

• In 1965 the average per capita income of those living in the Group of Seven rich democracies (G7) countries [the United States, Canada, Great Britain, Italy, France, Germany, and Japan] was 20 times that of those living in the world's poorest seven countries; 30 years later it was 39 times as much.

• The rate of return on capital in the business sectors of the G7 countries rose from 12.5 percent in the early 1980s to over 16 percent in the mid 90s, a development the United Nations Conference on Trade and Development (UNCTAD) calls, "the counterpart to declining wages."

• Public and private debt has risen in both developed and developing countries, with interest rates sometimes approaching 15 percent of Gross Domestic Product (GDP), a situation UNCTAD says has created "a new rentier class" generated by the "substantial" expansion of international capital flows and the hike in real interest rates.

Third World Poverty

Thus, the real world of corporate restructuring, labor shedding and wage repression where:

. . . 250 million of the world's children work in sweatshops;

. . . more than a billion people subsist on less than a dollar a day; nearly three times that many—three billion—live on less than two dollars;

. . . in the world's 48 least developed countries—with 10 percent of the world's population but only 1 percent of world income—both economic growth and trade have declined since 1980;

. . . more than nine million children in developing countries under the age of five die of avoidable causes each year;

. . . by the year 2000, half the population in sub-Saharan Africa will be living in absolute poverty;

. . . some 250 billionaires have a combined wealth equal to the annual incomes of nearly half of the world's people.

Approaches to Development

Such, then, is the "New World Order" where there is nothing new and little order but, rather, a brutal attempt by transnational capital, aided by compliant governments and the Bretton Woods institutions [the International Monetary Fund and the International Bank for Reconstruction and Development, created at the 1944 Bretton Woods Conference], to tighten the noose of exploitative relationships on the entire globe. Such is the new world order that ignores the Charter of Economic Rights, the Declaration on the Right to Development as well as Article 23 of the Universal Declaration of Human Rights.

Such is the new world order that is the grotesque opposite of the New International Economic Order adopted by the General Assembly on May 1, 1974 to "promote the economic advancement and social progress of all peoples" by establishing an economic order "based on equity, sovereign equality . . . common interest and cooperation between states . . . which shall correct inequalities and make it possible to eliminate the widening gap between the developed and developing countries."

If we say that sustainable human development is pro-people, pro-jobs and pro-nature—and that equal emphasis must be placed on each—then we must say something else: development patterns that perpetuate today's inequalities are neither sustainable nor worth sustaining.

The foundation of human development is that human life is valuable in itself. If we accept this—and none will admit differently—social development must be defined as development that improves the quality of life for the majority of humankind.

In our view, there can be no improvement in the quality of life for the 140 million people who are registered as unemployed unless a way is found to provide them with productive, meaningful jobs.

Nor can there be any improvement in the quality of life for the 30 percent of the world's three-billion-strong labor force who are under-employed unless jobs are created. And what about the 60 million young people between the ages of 15 and 24 who are in search of work and cannot find it? Certainly they—and the world's 1.1 billion people who live in absolute poverty—cannot even dream of a better life if present trends in economic and social development continue.

Liberal Policies Are Destructive

The 1997 Trade and Development Report says "some awkward truths" must be faced if the challenges of social development are to be met: "In the first place," UNCTAD said, "no economic law exists that will make developing economies converge automatically towards the income levels of developed countries. Second, growth and development do not automatically bring about a reduction in inequality."

The WFTU would add a third: a recognition that these tragic circumstances are not aberrations of a correct policy somehow gone wrong. Rather, they must be seen as a policy-induced disaster, the logical result of the anti-social content of the global policies of the transnational banks and corporations (TNCs), made worse by the conditionalities imposed by the World Bank and the International Monetary Fund.

The WFTU rejects any claim that current levels of un-

Corporations as Government

The nation-state is asked to play a subservient role to multi-national corporations; corporate rights are often more favorably treated than individual rights. Corporations have become aggressive in asserting their freedoms via "liberalization," overcoming government control through "deregulation," and taking over government activities through "privatization," according to [Philippine Green Party leader Roberto] Verzola.

Supra-national institutions such as the IMF, World Bank, and World Trade Organization are working to further negate national sovereignty through emerging global legal infrastructures; for example, the proposed Multilateral Agreement on Investment (MAI) would allow multinational corporations to dictate changes to a country's national, state, and local regulations governing labor, health, and environmental standards.

Anna Manzo, *Toward Freedom*, November 1998.

---

employment and under-employment are unavoidable components of modern society, unless of course, one equates "modern society" with the "market economy" or the "free enterprise system." Likewise we reject any idea that further liberalization of labor markets, diluting or eliminating international labor standards, forcing down real wages or working conditions will create additional employment opportunities.

The neo-liberal policies now in vogue have yet to yield positive results for workers and the people.

On the contrary, the rich have become richer and the poor poorer, while net capital transfers continue to deprive developing countries of development resources—a process which violates the right of development as well as the economic and social rights of the peoples of these countries.

Corporations Are Too Powerful

The WFTU believes that the current emphasis on deregulation, privatization and devaluing the role of the state sector, while dismantling the social security structures as advocated by neo-liberalism, is totally misplaced and can only invite a repetition of the crisis of the 1930s [the Great Depression]. And we are particularly concerned at liberalization measures which force developing and least-developed countries into unequal competition with transnational corporations (TNCs).

The TNCs not only dominate the most important banks and stock exchanges of the global financial system and control the availability of money and the terms under which loans are made, they control the prices of raw materials, high tech research and new technologies, particularly biotechnology, as well as the information and communication industries.

And they do more than dominate the global economy— they impose their ideology and culture on the peoples of the world. They sponsor "brain drain" where the best and the brightest leave their homeland and they also impose an international neocolonialist division of labor that, in essence, leaves things very much as they were when colonies became "independent" states.

Their domination will be further strengthened if negotiations for a Multilateral Agreement on Investment (MAI) succeed or if the attempts by some of the world's most powerful nations succeed in imposing changes that would transform the World Trade Organization (WTO) into a second International Monetary Fund (IMF).

It is with these concerns in mind that the WFTU calls for a review of the policies that have placed—and continue to place—the burden of the world's economic crisis on the backs of working people.

Policy Suggestions

We also wish to express our regrets that the work of framing a Code of Conduct governing activities of TNCs has been all but abandoned by the United Nations and why it strongly urges the Economic and Social Council to take appropriate steps to revisit that question and conclude work on a Code, and its adoption as an enforceable international instrument.

Given that the $1.5 trillion that moves on the world financial markets every day creates no value and adds nothing to the wealth of nations, it is our position that the UN, as representative of the international community, should take appropriate measures to dampen currency speculation by the application of a tax on each transaction, the proceeds of which could be used to finance social development in the world's poor nations. Such a tax, called the "Tobin Tax," was first proposed by a professor from Yale.

And finally, we find it difficult to understand why there has been no serious action toward implementing the Ten Commitments of the Copenhagen Declaration, which include elimination of absolute poverty, support for full employment, equality between men and women, acceleration of the development of Africa and the least developed countries and attain universal access to education and primary health care as agreed to at the World Summit for Social Development (WSSD).

We suggest that, too, become a question near the top of the international agenda.

We hold, in the words of the Alternative Declaration adopted by the Caucus of Non-governmental Organizations at the WSSD, that "we are at a point of leaving our children a world in which we, ourselves, would not wish to live.

But we do find tremendous inspiration and hope in the fact that . . . we can draw from the present crisis the creativity to make a world community that truly works."

That is the overarching responsibility of the United Nations as representative of the peoples of the world which speaks for them on the world's stage and in its centers of power.

"In the poorest countries, debt repayments divert scarce financial resources from social investments necessary for sustainable development."

Debt Relief or Cancellation Will Aid Third World Development

Roger Mahony

In the following viewpoint, Roger Mahony, the cardinal archbishop of the Roman Catholic archdiocese of Los Angeles, asserts that Third World nations cannot develop their economies unless they are given debt relief. Mahony claims that more money is spent by developing nations on debt repayment than on health care and education. He suggests that the year 2000 would be an ideal time to begin debt relief. In June 1999, the leaders of the Group of Seven rich democracies—the United States, Canada, Great Britain, Italy, France, Germany, and Japan—agreed to write off debts for thirty-six nations totaling $70 billion.

As you read, consider the following questions:
1. How much did developing nations owe their creditors in 1995, as cited by Mahony?
2. In the author's view, who shares the responsibility for the debt situation?
3. According to Mahony, what should be the goals of future loans?

Excerpted from "The Cost of International Debt in Human Terms," by Roger Mahony, *Origins*, November 20, 1997. Reprinted with permission.

The topic I have chosen for our gathering may have taken some by surprise. Third World debt is not exactly a subject one might hear discussed around the breakfast table. All of us are keenly aware of the immediate pressures which weigh heavily on families in our own communities:

- Violence in our neighborhoods and in the home.
- Disparities in wealth and income that leave many in poverty.
- Access to adequate health care, and
- The quality of our educational system.

So, given these issues which may seem more imminent, why do we focus on the topic of Third World debt?

We turn our attention to international debt in order to reaffirm our commitment to work with our sisters and brothers in developing countries who struggle to escape from under the weight of their country's debt burden.

The Impact of Debts

For many in the Third World, their country's staggering foreign debt is one of the most crippling economic impediments to securing the basics which make life dignified: food, housing, education and health care.

As the bishops of Africa wrote in 1994:

"Africa is home to hundreds of millions of the poorest people on earth. They are shackled with a burden of unpayable debt, which is both a symptom and a cause of their poverty. It is a symptom because they would not have borrowed if they were not poor; it is a cause because the crushing burden of debt repayments makes them poorer still."

In the poorest countries, debt repayments divert scarce financial resources from social investments necessary for sustainable development: health care, schools, food production for domestic consumption, environmental protection and preservation, and other key foundations of the social infrastructure.

The scope and impact of the external debt of developing nations is staggering. Consider these figures:

- As of 1995, developing nations owed foreign creditors in excess of $2 trillion.
- Thirty-five of the world's poorest countries owed $226

billion in 1995—less than the U.S. fiscal year 1998 defense budget. Twenty-eight of these countries are in Africa.

- In 1995, the cumulative debt of sub-Saharan Africa, excluding South Africa and Namibia, was $199 billion—a figure that is 20 percent higher than these countries' total income.
- Arrears—the portion of the debt that cannot be paid—account for one-third of Africa's total debt. In 1994 alone, African countries paid $11 billion to service their debt. This, however, was only half of the $22 billion they needed to pay in order to stay current for that year.
- Between 1990 and 1993, Mozambique was able to make only 10 percent of its scheduled payments, adding approximately $570 million to its debt stock. As a result of the debt payments the government was able to make, staples of the social infrastructure like health care and schooling have suffered dramatically. Malaria, measles and acute respiratory infections account for 50 percent of in-hospital child deaths—all treatable conditions! Outbreaks of dysentery, diarrhea and cholera are compounded by the fact that only one-third of the rural population has potable drinking water or sufficient caloric intake.

The Example of Mozambique

In 1994, Mozambique made only 20 percent of its scheduled payments. Yet this amount represented:

- More than double the amount of recurrent expenditures in the education sector.
- More than four times the recurrent expenditures in the health sector; and
- More than the recurrent budgets for health, education, police and judicial systems combined.

As a result, out of Mozambique's total population of between 16 million and 18 million people:

- Ten million do not have safe drinking water.
- Two-thirds of the adults are illiterate; two-thirds of those are women.
- One million children do not attend primary schools.

- Nine million do not have access to the formal health system.
- Each year 190,000 children die before their fifth birthday.
- Over 10,000 women die each year from childbirth-related complications.

These figures barely begin to illustrate the toll that debt service exacts on the people of developing nations. But they are the foundation of a moral argument for the reduction or cancellation of debt. When children go hungry or die from preventable diseases, when potable drinking water is not available, when more is spent on debt service than on health care and education, then the cost of debt, in human terms, is unjustified.

Proclaiming a Jubilee Year

In 1994, Pope John Paul II issued the apostolic letter titled *Tertio Millennio Adveniente*, "As the Third Millennium Draws Near." In it he stated that "a commitment to justice and peace in a world like ours, marked by so many conflicts and intolerable social and economic inequalities, is a necessary condition for the preparation and celebration of the jubilee. Thus, in the spirit of Leviticus (25:8–12), Christians will have to raise their voice on behalf of all the poor of the world, proposing the jubilee as an appropriate time to give thought, among other things, to reducing substantially, if not canceling outright, the international debt which threatens the future of many nations."

In the Jewish and Christian traditions, the jubilee year fell every 50 years. The Book of Leviticus tells us that "you shall hallow the 50th year and proclaim liberty throughout the land to all its inhabitants; it shall be a jubilee year for you, when each of you shall return to his property and each of you shall return to his family" (Lv. 25:10).

The jubilee year was a time of renewal and emancipation. It was an opportunity to mend broken relationships, to reconcile the community to God and to rectify the condition of the poor.

It is in this light that the "jubilee year was meant to restore equality among all the children of Israel, offering new possibilities to families which had lost their property and even their personal freedom. . . . The jubilee year was a reminder to the rich that a time would come when their Israelite slaves would once again become their equals and would be able to reclaim their rights."

The church's advocacy for the reduction or cancellation of Third World debt emerges from its abiding concern for the poor. The preferential option for the poor, which is a central principle of the church's social tradition, is deeply rooted in the prophetic writings of the Hebrew Scriptures. The prophets remind us that the quality of justice in the land and the integrity of the community's relationship with God is measured by how the poor, the widow, the orphan and the alien are treated. Throughout the Hebrew Scriptures, right worship and fidelity to the covenant relationship with God are judged by the community's treatment of the poor and marginalized.

Debt Relief Is Necessary

The debt crisis calls on us to reaffirm our solidarity with the poor in developing countries through a call for debt relief.

Those in economic and financial circles may all too easily dismiss this "jubilee talk" of forgiving Third World debt as reckless banter. This would be both unfortunate and shortsighted. Contrary to what some opponents of debt relief may say, there is neither the expectation nor the desire for the World Bank and other international financial institutions to close their doors come January in the year 2000. Quite the contrary, the World Bank, its partner institutions and creditor nations each share responsibility for the current situation of unsustainable debt. Each, therefore, should take active leadership in working with debtor nations to devise just and humane solutions for relieving the debt burden. It is in this spirit that the Pontifical Justice and Peace Commission wrote that "the burden (for resolving the debt crisis) should not fall disproportionately on poor countries. . . . It is morally wrong to deprive a nation of the means to meet the basic needs of its people in order to repay debt."

To those who dismiss debt relief as unrealistic, I would ask: Are banks and Northern economies realistic if they expect the current crisis to continue along without disastrous implications? Is it realistic for creditors to expect debtor nations to meet the complicated steps and requirements of the Heavily Indebted Poor Country Initiative that leave many worthy candidates for debt reduction or cancellation with little hope of relief in the near or midterm? Is it realistic for creditors to stubbornly cling to an economic approach and philosophy that has impoverished so many people in so many countries?

Debtor Countries Cannot Develop

Countries have responsibilities in addition to servicing their debts, including meeting the needs of the poor, which in many Third World countries constitute the bulk of the population. These other responsibilities would be protected in an international bankruptcy court. Local governments in the U.S., such as Orange County, California, can receive protection from their creditors through the courts. Under current international arrangements, creditors require payment, regardless of the effect on the poor.

Under today's conditions, poor countries are unable to get on with the business of development. Debtor governments cannot hope to attract investors; heavy indebtedness indicates to the investor that the country is not a good investment risk. In addition, poor countries' few skilled civil servants are tied up in endless rounds of debt renegotiations instead of long-term planning for resolving poverty.

Jo Marie Griesgraber, *Christian Century*, January 22, 1997.

Mr. Wolfensohn and his colleagues at the World Bank who are committed to debt relief for poor countries face a daunting challenge. Not the least of these obstacles is the reluctance of creditor nations like the United States to seriously commit to debt relief. It is the creditor nations who sponsor the World Bank who have insisted upon layers of requirements and protracted time lines which effectively quash the hope of debt relief for the vast majority of the heavily indebted poor countries. They, however, also have the power to change these requirements. The spirit of the Heavily Indebted Poor Country Initiative must not be crushed by stringent and, in some cases, unobtainable requirements.

As the Catholic bishops of the United States stated in 1989, past efforts to address the debt issue were short-term in nature and designed primarily to protect creditors and the financial system. With the debt crisis now clear to all, it is time for new initiatives guided by an ethic which places highest priority on the human and moral consequences of any new debt-relief proposals.

How to Reduce Debt

I would encourage the World Bank to work with its government sponsors—and, when necessary, to pressure and cajole them—to ensure a "rapid application of new debt reduction terms to the widest number of countries" by the year 2000.

Some may argue that the World Bank, the International Monetary Fund and other international financial institutions should not interfere with the policies and prerogatives of sovereign states (when referring to creditor nations). But one must remember that macroeconomic reforms such as those required by structural adjustment policies seek to intervene in debtor countries in ways that developed nations would find intolerable.

Initiatives such as the Mauritius Mandate* outlined by the United Kingdom in September 1997 demonstrate the type of leadership possible on the issue of debt cancellation and in setting expeditious time lines for debt reduction.

The current debt overhang limits growth by discouraging foreign private investment and by diverting foreign aid from domestic investment to debt service. Private investors are more likely to invest in developing nations that are made more secure and stable due to canceled or significantly reduced foreign debt. Foreign aid, in turn, would be more effective when used for social investments rather than debt repayment.

Future loans should be scrutinized carefully to ensure that they further the goals of human development. In other words, will future debt protect human life, promote human

---

* British Chancellor Gordon Brown announced the Mauritius Mandate at the September 1997 Commonwealth Finance Ministers summit in Mauritania. It is Britain's policy on debt, and the proposal is centered on reducing the debt burden for twenty nations in Africa and South America.

dignity, foster an economic system in which participation and inclusion are inviolable characteristics and encourage stewardship of natural resources?

In the same vein, debt relief should include agreements between creditors and debtors that the money saved through a reduction or cancellation in debt service will be converted into funding for health care, sanitation, education, food and the like. These "social conditionalities" should be determined with the full participation of people in those countries. It is along these lines that creditor nations should take up the United Kingdom's challenge, again outlined in the Mauritius Mandate, to suspend programs for Heavily Indebted Poor Country Initiative countries such as export credit guarantees for arm sales. These subsidies make it easier for developing countries to buy armaments than food.

The Role of Religious Groups

The demands of solidarity in an increasingly globalized world argue for Third World debt to be a concern for all of us. Creditor nations like the United States and international financial institutions like the World Bank represent each of us in the global economy. The moral imperative of this situation impels us to call on these creditors and institutions to reassess their current criteria for debt reduction to allow more nations to qualify more quickly for debt relief and, hopefully in some cases, cancellation of debt.

The Catholic Church is certainly not alone in its concern for the poor. But as an institution with a 2,000-year history, we seize this moment on an issue of great urgency. Mr. Wolfensohn, the Catholic Church does not agree with World Bank policies in every area. We do, however, applaud the efforts which the World Bank has undertaken under your unflagging leadership to put this issue of debt relief on the table. Yet, there is still much more to be done before the bold vision of the Heavily Indebted Poor Country Initiative touches the lives of men, women and children in Mozambique, Zambia, Zimbabwe, Honduras, Nicaragua and other countries with unsustainable debt. The success of debt relief initiatives will be measured by the degree to which the lives of persons in those countries are improved. . . .

In closing, I would ask us to prayerfully consider the words of Pope John Paul II when he asked:

"Is it merely a rhetorical question to ask how many infants and children die every day in Africa because resources are now being swallowed up in debt repayment? There is no time to lament policies of the past or those elements in the international financial picture which have led up to the present situation. Now it is the time for a new and courageous international solidarity, a solidarity not based in self-interest but inspired and guided by a true concern for human beings."

"It is by no means obvious that debt cancellation would enable [poor countries] to start all over again."

Debt Cancellation Will Not Aid Third World Development

Martin Vander Weyer

Writing off the debts of Third World nations will not necessarily aid their development, Martin Vander Weyer contends in the following viewpoint. He argues that overgenerous debt relief would reward countries that wasted their resources and punish developing nations that have struggled to pay off their debts. Vander Weyer also asserts that private investments are not likely to increase after debt cancellation because developing nations have a poor track record at borrowing money. Vander Weyer is a book reviewer and commentator for the *London Telegraph*.

As you read, consider the following questions:
1. What is the ratio of debt payments to foreign aid, according to the author?
2. In Vander Weyer's view, why should debt relief not be compared with bankruptcy procedures?
3. What approach does the author suggest for debt relief?

Excerpted from "It's a Bad Idea, Bono, So Don't Give Up the Day Job: Writing Off Third World Debts Would Not Help Those Most in Need," by Martin Vander Weyer, *Sunday Telegraph*, February 21, 1999. Reprinted with the permission of Martin Vander Weyer.

Oh Lord, spare us from the preposterous preaching of rock- and film-star riff-raff, fooled by fame into thinking they have some kind of moral authority. [In February 1999], timed to coincide with the Brit Awards [a British music awards ceremony], we were treated to a particularly crass and ill-informed sermon from Bono, the Irish-born lead singer of U2, on the subject of why the West should write off the debts of the Third World.

"As a pop star I have two instincts," he began a rambling essay in *The Guardian*. "I want to have fun. And I want to change the world." To judge from this effort, he probably has more success at the former than the latter, though over the years he has lent his name to a colourful variety of causes—he is a veteran of Bob Geldof's 1985 Live Aid concert, and made an on-stage appearance last year with Messrs Trimble and Hume in support of the Irish peace process. Despite his stream-of-consciousness prose, the effect of his intervention will be to concertina a complex debate, so it appears there is only one side that anyone with a trace of fashionable concern could possibly take.

The Debt Reduction Bandwagon

It really isn't that simple, Mr Bono (or may I call you by your real name, Paul Hewson). Both morally and politically, this is a difficult issue. But you have jumped on a crowded bandwagon, already occupied by the Pope, the Dalai Lama, Salman Rushdie, Muhammad Ali and Gordon Brown. Your presence with them in support of the "Jubilee 2000" campaign confirms debt relief as the pre-millennial issue for a broad spectrum of rock fans, student radicals, trade unionists, Christians and aid campaigners: all those who believe, with you, that "the rule of money-lenders has gone too far".

You can even claim intellectual support from the Right, quoting both Jeffrey Sachs, the Harvard free-marketeer, and the Adam Smith Institute. According to the institute, cancellation of unpayable debt will not only "raise the living standards of the desperately poor but . . . give them the chance and the investment to embark on that upward path which generates growth, wealth and jobs. Cancellation is in our interests as well as theirs".

With such a galaxy of support, the moral basis for debt forgiveness seems almost as unanswerable as the case against apartheid which united most of the same groups 20 years ago. Sub-Saharan Africa, for example, owes more than pounds 135 billion to Western creditors, who take back pounds 5 in debt payments for every pounds 2 they offer in aid (these are Jubilee 2000's figures, but Bono puts the ratio at pounds 9 of debt service to pounds 1 of aid—hey, what do numbers matter when you're trying to change the world?). Cancellation of those debts would, campaigners say, save the lives of 20 million children by 2000—and provide basic education for 90 million women, reducing infant mortality rates for many years to come.

Underlying this claim is the example of Ethiopia, which spends almost half its export earnings on debt service and four times as much on debt as on health care, while 10,000 Ethiopian children die each year of preventable diseases. Attention has also focused on Honduras and Nicaragua, which were ordered by the International Monetary Fund (IMF) last year to keep paying their debts (at pounds 1 million per day) at a time when 800,000 of their citizens had their livelihoods destroyed by Hurricane Mitch.

Storm, drought, crop failure, war or maladministration has reduced these countries to a state of human despair in which it seems pompous, un-Christian, perhaps even barking mad, to insist that a debt stands as a stain on the character of the debtor until it is paid. The ground-rules of bourgeois capitalism inhabit a lower moral order than the principles of charity, which certainly require us to save lives first.

These are the arguments sketched by Pope John Paul [II] in his 1994 apostolic letter, and developed by Cardinal Hume* at the launch of Jubilee 2000, when he called on political leaders to achieve "something of lasting benefit to the human family". They are now bandied about by the likes of Bono with the emotional volume of a Wembley concert. The counter-arguments are shouted down, but in fact they are reasonable and humane.

*Cardinal Basil Hume was the leader of the Roman Catholic Church of England and Wales. He died on June 17, 1999.

There are, first of all, sound moral and practical reasons why state debts should be cancelled only as a very last resort and in a closely controlled way, rather than by the sweeping gesture proposed by Jubilee 2000. These are debts to Western Governments and organisations such as the IMF, rather than to private-sector banks, so there is no "shareholder greed" involved. Lenders may share the blame for the failure of the loans to generate sufficient economic activity to enable them to be repaid normally, but that blame must lie chiefly with the borrowers—ministers who spent the money on "showpiece" projects which failed, or on guns, or on themselves and their Swiss bank accounts.

Dick Wright © *Providence Journal Bulletin*. Distributed by the Los Angeles Times Syndicate. Reprinted with permission.

How many more lives would be saved, we might ask, by a moratorium on arms buying, rather than a moratorium on debt? Over-generous debt relief would merely encourage a cycle of irresponsibility and corruption, offering the biggest rewards to those regimes which have wasted their resources most thoroughly. It would reward the war-lords who terrorise central Africa. It would penalise poor countries such as Bangladesh, which have struggled to maintain a respectable debt record, and those such as Uganda and Mozambique, which have gone through years of hardship to qualify for partial relief under the existing Highly Indebted Poor Countries (HIPC) scheme devised by the World Bank.

And it would send a strange message to private citizens. The world's economic system depends on universal understanding of the concept of debt. There are millions of people now finding their own path out of abject poverty by borrowing from "micro-credit" institutions modelled on Muhammad Yunus's Grameen Bank in Bangladesh, which has a 99 per cent success rate in collecting repayments. Those people, borrowing pounds 30 or pounds 50 to buy a cow or a rickshaw, understand not only their own obligation to repay, but the fact that, in Grameen' s system, if they fail to repay, others in their community will not be able to borrow. However limited their economic sphere, they are treated as responsible participants in a global system. What are they to think if whole nations are treated as children, told that they can forget their debts? Jubilee campaigners for debt relief say that such nations can indeed be treated like children—because their most important citizens are, in fact, starving children. They also make comparisons with bankruptcy procedures for private citizens, who are able, after an interval, to start again with a clean slate. But no one has ever attempted to revive a poor town by declaring all its residents, whatever their remaining resources and prospects, bankrupt at the same time.

Part of the tragedy of the poor countries' situation is that it is by no means obvious that debt cancellation would enable them to start all over again. Private sector investors will not be attracted by the risks of countries with a track record of total failure as past borrowers. Bono is wrong to say that cancelling debt was what helped a devastated post-war Germany back to economic health: it was the fact that German negotiators, lead by the banker Herman Abs, agreed to shoulder a burden of past debt that enabled Germany to rejoin the international financial community.

And Bono—a resident, and presumably a taxpayer, of Ireland—does not seem to have considered the weight of opinion of fellow taxpayers in western countries more prominent than Ireland in Third World aid and lending. The Group of

Seven (G7) Governments [the United States, Canada, Great Britain, France, Germany, Italy, and Japan] are increasingly under pressure from their voters to keep taxes low, so unlikely to be generous to the world's poor next time round. Campaigners argue that the debts which are so damaging to the world's poor are as nothing to the G7 rich: "How many British taxpayers would die if we forgave Sudan the pounds 170 million it owes us?", they ask. Well, pounds 170 million may not be much, but it would still pay for a 500-bed hospital in one of Britain's poorest cities. If the flow of pounds 5 debt service payments which might eventually have repaid it has been cancelled, who will feel inclined to send pounds 2 of aid in the other direction?

Looked at another way, that five-to-two formula identified by Jubilee 2000 already represents a well-targeted method of relieving two-fifths of the debt. It reminds us that the best mechanism of debt relief is one which redirects debt payments straight into healthcare and poverty reduction— through sustainable farming and irrigation projects, for example. Conducted on a limited scale, this can be monitored by international bodies. Write off an entire national debt, however, and there will be no control at all over who gets the benefit. Inevitably, in corrupt, war-torn territories, it will not be the poor.

Debt Relief Is Unlikely

But it just isn't going to happen anyway. When President Clinton "toured" Africa (touching down briefly at a handful of African airports) [in 1998], he barely paid lip service to the subject of debt relief. At May [1998's] G8 [G7 and Russia] meeting in Birmingham, besieged by Jubilee 2000 protesters, Tony Blair failed to promote agreement on measures to broaden the HIPC scheme. During Hurricane Mitch, only the French made any concrete gesture towards instant debt relief for afflicted countries. There is too dangerous a financial principle at stake for any government to agree wholeheartedly to Jubilee 2000's proposals. Blair and Brown may posture on the subject, but they are safe in the knowledge that the United States will always veto large-scale reform, and will take the international blame.

This means that all those worthy campaigners are wasting valuable energy and moral indignation, when they could be working for the good of the poor in other ways. If Bono really feels for the starving of Africa, he should shut up and write a very large cheque to Oxfam or Care. He should not try to whip up popular emotion on a subject he clearly doesn't understand.

<cut here>VIEWPOINT 5

"The World Bank's purpose is to help borrowers reduce poverty and improve living standards through sustainable growth and investment in people."

The World Bank Provides Effective Development Programs

The World Bank

In its 1998 annual report, the World Bank maintains that its programs, including loans, reduce poverty and improve living standards in developing countries. The World Bank contends that partnerships with governmental and nongovernmental organizations will further increase its effectiveness. The World Bank is an institution owned by more than 180 member countries whose views are represented by a Board of Governors and Board of Directors. The organization raises money through contributions from member governments and the world's capital markets and uses those funds to aid over one hundred developing nations as of June 1999.

As you read, consider the following questions:
1. According to the World Bank, what factors allowed for greater opportunity for development in Africa?
2. In the organization's view, what is the key to effective development?
3. What is the central tenet of the World Bank's role?

Excerpted from the overview of the World Bank's *Annual Report 1998*, available at www.worldbank.org/html/pic/PIC.html. This material is edited from the original and reprinted with the permission of The World Bank (The World Bank cannot be held responsible for the accuracy of this information.) The complete and original version of this material can be accessed via the above web site or a print copy requested from The World Bank Infoshop, 1818 H St. NW, Rm. J1-060, Washington, DC, or pic@worldbank.org).

The World Bank's purpose is to help borrowers reduce poverty and improve living standards through sustainable growth and investment in people. In fiscal 1998, the Bank made strong headway in implementing the Strategic Compact, aimed at increasing development impact and playing its part in the fight against poverty more effectively. The Board of Executive Directors reviewed two progress reports on the compact in fiscal 1998 that documented improvements in the quality, timeliness, and quantity of operational work, and in organization, processes, and ways of doing business.

Responding to Crises

The Bank's renewed capacity to deliver high-quality services through effective partnerships was tested in fiscal 1998 in its ability to respond to a new challenge—the East Asian financial crisis, which speeded up the pace of change across the institution—and in the strong turnaround in the performance of the Africa region, which had been the starting place of the Bank's renewal program.

Following the dramatic downturn in financial markets in several East Asian countries early in the fiscal year, the Bank moved quickly to adjust both lending programs and advisory services. The crisis risks undermining one of the most remarkable economic achievements of the twentieth century—and perhaps the single most effective antipoverty performance in history. As an institution whose core mandate is poverty reduction, the Bank helped support the international effort to restore confidence and sustainable growth by focusing on both the financial and the human dimensions of the crisis—including unemployment, food shortages, and the effects on the poorest and most vulnerable groups.

The Bank pledged some $16 billion to support reform programs in the countries facing critical situations, of which $5.65 billion was disbursed. This included a $3,000 million loan to the Republic of Korea, the largest loan in the Bank's history, which was processed in record time.

The East Asian crisis underscored the prudence of the Bank's renewed financial sector emphasis under the Strategic Compact. As the East Asian financial crisis rapidly escalated, the Bank geared up to respond quickly and credibly.

Additional resources were approved to reinforce the financial sector program, and the Special Financial Operations Unit was established to help respond to the crisis in all affected countries, not just in East Asia, by providing support to help its clients strengthen weak financial systems and reduce the impact of the crisis on poor and other vulnerable people. Staff capacity was built up through recruitment; collaboration and coordination with external partners were enhanced, including with the new Financial Sector Advisory Service established with the help of a Policy and Human Resources Development (PHRD) grant, and with European donors through the Asia-Europe Meeting (ASEM) Trust Fund; and a Central Bank secondment program was established in several countries.

The international effort consisted of close partnerships—from other multilateral institutions, particularly the International Monetary Fund (IMF), and with nongovernmental organizations (NGOs). Working in close coordination with the IMF, for example, the Bank promptly organized a series of technical assistance missions to assist the governments of Indonesia, the Republic of Korea, and Thailand—including helping to identify and address problems in the financial and corporate sectors.

Debts in Africa

While addressing new challenges to meet the needs of client countries facing crises in East Asia, the Bank and its African clients began to reap the rewards of stronger partnerships and closer client focus.

Continued growth, improved economic policies, and increased political openness in many parts of the region, together with a new generation of African leaders, created greater opportunity for development in the region. Lending commitments to Africa increased by almost two thirds to $2,873.8 million after fiscal 1997's downturn, reflecting significant policy improvements in some African countries and the completion of the Bank's renewal process, which had delayed the pace of commitments in fiscal 1997. At $2,506 million, disbursements also remained high.

The Bank's focus on working more closely with client

partners was exemplified in Africa in fiscal 1998. The Bank's president participated in two key meetings in Kampala and Dakar with African leaders where he learned from them firsthand about their development priorities and how the Bank could best help meet them.

The special needs of Africa's heavily indebted countries progressed as Uganda became the first country to reach its completion point under the Heavily Indebted Poor Countries (HIPC) Debt Initiative in April 1998, when the Boards of Executive Directors of the IMF and IDA agreed that the necessary conditions had been fulfilled. The Bank's assistance was provided in the form of grants for education, purchase and cancellation of outstanding debt owed to IDA, and servicing debt owed to IDA over the next five years. Decisions to provide assistance under the initiative were taken for three African countries (Burkina Faso, Côte d'Ivoire, and Mozambique) and two South American countries (Bolivia and Guyana). Eligibility for the initiative was reviewed for four more African countries with Guinea-Bissau and Mali expected to receive HIPC debt relief, while the debt situations for Benin and Senegal were confirmed sustainable after the full application of existing debt relief mechanisms.

Both the World Bank and IMF remain committed to meeting their full shares of the cost of the initiative. The IBRD'S Board of Governors approved the transfer of $250 million from IBRD surplus and net income to the HIPC Debt Initiative Trust Fund, the principle vehicle through which the Bank will deliver its debt relief. The IMF has provided service debt relief (sdr) of $250 million to its Enhanced Structural Assistance Facility (esaf)-HIPC Trust to finance special esaf operations under the initiative and approved an additional transfer of sdr $40 million. In addition, fifteen bilateral donors made contributions or pledges of about $275 million to the HIPC Trust Fund to assist other multilateral creditors (including the African Development Bank Group) in providing their respective shares of debt relief to qualifying hipcs.

External Events

[In 1998], several East Asian and African nations, along with some Latin American countries, were among those confronted by another external event that caused them to turn to the Bank and its partners for urgent support: the severe weather conditions resulting from El Niño oscillation. Several governments anticipated damage and disaster and requested the Bank's help to prepare themselves. Partnership with the Inter-American Development Bank (IDB), the United States Agency for International Development (USAID), and the United States National Oceanic and Atmospheric Administration (NOAA), together with the Bank's streamlined procedures, helped facilitate speedy responses to these requests for help. A seminar held in collaboration with the Bank's Environment Department, the Economic Development Institute (EDI), and the International START Secretariat provided a forum for participants from governments, NGOs, the private sector, and others to plan for long-term activities to mitigate the impact of drought induced by El Niño.

Supporting reconstruction after conflict remained a major activity in several countries, including Angola, Bosnia and Herzegovina, Rwanda, and Tajikistan.

Effective Development

The Bank is committed to the development targets adopted by the international community for improving the lives and environment of people who live in its client countries. While more people in its client countries are healthier, better fed, and more educated than ever before, progress is uneven among countries, and much more needs to be done. Increasing its development effectiveness lies at the heart of the Bank's renewal. Evaluations completed in fiscal 1998 showed steady improvements. Bank operations achieved better results, portfolio quality was improved, and evaluation processes were enhanced but indicated that continued progress in meeting the development effectiveness goals set out in the Strategic Compact will depend on current efforts to sustain and strengthen the portfolio. The Annual Report on Portfolio Performance (ARPP) showed improvement in the overall portfolio performance as both actual and potential problem projects declined from 31 percent of the portfolio to 26 percent by commitment value and from 34 percent to 30 percent by number of projects.

The Bank's strategic underpinning for refocusing the development agenda to improve development effectiveness is the country assistance strategy (CAS), the centerpiece of Bank-government interaction. A CAS evaluation report prepared in fiscal 1998 documented improvements in CASs, and identified three priorities for further advances: sharper strategic selectivity, more candid treatment of risks, and enhanced self-evaluation and monitoring of CAS implementation. Improvements were evident in two directions: increased client focus and strategic selectivity.

Development Lessons

What we as a development community can do is help countries by providing financing, yes; but even more important, by providing knowledge and lessons learned about the challenges and how to address them.

We must learn to let go. We must accept that the projects we fund are not donor projects or World Bank projects—they are Costa Rican projects, or Bangladeshi projects, or Chinese projects. And, development projects and programs must be fully owned by stakeholders if they are to succeed. We must listen to those stakeholders.

Second, our partnerships must be inclusive—involving bilaterals and multilaterals, the U.N., the European Union, regional organizations, the WTO, labor organizations, NGOs, foundations, and the private sector. With each of us playing to our respective strengths, we can leverage up the entire development effort.

James D. Wolfensohn, *Vital Speeches of the Day*, October 15, 1997.

Mainstreaming the social dimensions of development is key to effective and sustainable development, and some 125 social assessments were completed or underway in fiscal 1998. Regional social development action plans were prepared, and resources for social development were provided under the Strategic Compact. An increasing number of CASs paid special attention to social development issues, and the involvement of key stakeholders in the preparation process of many also helped meet social objectives.

The goals and targets of the Rural Development Action Plan, approved in fiscal 1997, also are supported under the

Strategic Compact. Initiatives in support of the plan included development of rural strategy papers for Guinea, Madagascar, Mali, and Uganda; dissemination of a rural development and water strategy in Morocco and Yemen and development of a rural water strategy for Tunisia; and initiation of a regional rural development strategy for South Asia and of sector studies on agricultural marketing and land markets in Sri Lanka.

Creating Partnerships

The important role that partnerships are playing in reinforcing the Bank's development activities and enhancing development effectiveness is illustrated throughout the pages of [the World Bank] Annual Report. The Partnership Group was established in fiscal 1998 to help build and facilitate further partnerships to make the Bank a more efficient player in development.

A central tenet of the evolving role of the World Bank is to build it into a world-class knowledge institution through a knowledge management system that extends across the World Bank and outside to mobilize knowledge and learning for better results. Underpinning this effort in fiscal 1998 was an action plan for consolidating information management and technology systems to ensure that individual Bank units' efforts align with institutional priorities. Prototype knowledge management systems in education and health were established, and a common framework for the systems was set up in the Bank's regional offices.

While the regional offices' knowledge management efforts focused on developing country-level information and live databases, the thematic networks began implementing a knowledge management program in fifteen sectors (such as education, finance, health, infrastructure, and poverty), with information being compiled around eighty "knowledge domains." Work began on establishing a community of practice for each topic, which includes help desks, advisory services, a directory of expertise, collections of statistics and information about the Bank's operations and activities, and collections of know-how emphasizing best practices and lessons learned. Provision is being made for external clients to access the system.

The Bank helps to facilitate learning and strengthen client country capacity through EDI's activities. As greater emphasis has been placed on knowledge as a catalyst of reform, EDI's role has increased. In fiscal 1998 the efficiency of EDI's services was improved and its reach extended: some 23,250 direct participants, including national leaders, government officials, parliamentarians, journalists, private entrepreneurs, NGOs, and educators were reached through 402 EDI learning activities. Partnerships within the Bank were strengthened: with the Bank's thematic networks, for example, EDI launched and piloted core courses on development priorities from banking, finance, and regulation to environment and sustainable development and from governance to human and social development. These courses help spread up-to-the-minute knowledge on key development challenges. To integrate client training programs into overall development efforts, EDI provided program support, on a selective basis, in the preparation of twelve CASs in fiscal 1998.

The Global Distance Education network, established in fiscal 1998, is using interactive television, videoconferencing, and the Internet to deliver training and policy services to more development partners than is possible through face-to-face learning. An interactive electronic classroom was set up in the Bank's Main Complex, and core courses are being converted to distance education delivery.

The cost effectiveness review (CER) was completed and endorsed by the Board of Executive Directors in October 1997, and implementation began. The CER implementation is leading to changes in systems and procedures to deliver better services while realizing estimated potential savings in fiscal 1999 through fiscal 2001. These changes, targeting higher productivity in the frontline and generating savings through efficiency gains in the backline, are on track to realize the Strategic Compact's goal of having frontline resources account for 60 percent of the budget while support activities account for 40 percent by fiscal 1999.

To help make the budget an instrument of the Bank's strategy and link resource allocation more closely with institutional priorities, a new more strategic and transparent planning and budgeting process was developed at a strategic forum held in January 1998. Among the outcomes of the forum were:

- agreement on five Bank Group-wide corporate priorities;
- an intensified action program for implementing the internal renewal program; and
- budget allocation principles designed to align resources better with corporate priorities.

Bank management and the Board of Executive Directors monitored progress in reaching the objectives set out in the Strategic Compact to maximize the Bank's effectiveness in the fight against poverty.

In fiscal 1998 the Board of Executive Directors endorsed reform of the Bank's human resources policies to align them with the needs of the new Bank. The new strategy will help the Bank attract and retain the best people from all over the world, treat them fairly over the course of their Bank careers, and foster teamwork, learning, and innovation.

> "*After nearly three decades, it seems clear*
> *that most long-term recipients of World*
> *Bank loans still are not achieving*
> *'sustainable development.'*"

The World Bank Does Not Provide Effective Development Programs

Bryan T. Johnson

In the following viewpoint, Bryan T. Johnson argues that the World Bank has not improved living standards in less developed countries. He asserts that the majority of nations that have received World Bank loans have either failed to improve their economic prospects or are now worse off than they were prior to the loans. According to Johnson, these countries fail to develop because they lack economic freedom. Johnson is a policy analyst for the Heritage Foundation, a conservative public policy research organization, and the coauthor of the Heritage Foundation/*Wall Street Journal* Index of Economic Freedom.

As you read, consider the following questions:
1. What was the World Bank's primary mission when it was founded, according to the author?
2. According to statistics cited by Johnson, how many of the countries that have received funds from the World Bank for at least twenty-five years have had their economies decreased by at least 20 percent?
3. How many long-term recipients of World Bank aid have "free" economies, in Johnson's opinion?

Excerpted from "The World Bank and Economic Growth: Fifty Years of Failure," by Bryan T. Johnson, *Heritage Foundation Backgrounder*, May 16, 1996. Reprinted with the permission of The Heritage Foundation.

The World Bank has undergone a major transformation since it started in 1944. The Bank claims it has kept up with change to deal with the new challenges facing less developed countries. This contention is debatable, but it is true that the fundamental mission today is substantially different from what it was in 1944.

Early Lending Policies

In the beginning, the Bank's primary mission was to loan money to the war-ravaged countries of Western Europe and Japan to help them get on their feet after World War II. These loans were intended to help rebuild roads, bridges, electrical plants, and other public facilities and enterprises. Japan and the European countries would use World Bank loans when private bank loans were not forthcoming. Many private commercial banks refused to lend these nations money because they were bad risks, some of them having defaulted on World War I and post-World War I debts.

From 1944 to the mid-1950s, most World Bank loans went to the developed countries in Europe that had suffered extensive damage in World War II. Therefore, even though the Bank loaned some $543 million for the reconstruction of Europe, the money was absorbed by countries that essentially were advanced developed economies with strong economic foundations in banking, property rights protection, the rule of law, functioning courts, and borders open to foreign investment.

Because these countries already had the basic building blocks of an advanced economy, they were able to put the World Bank loans to productive use. Yet U.S. private investment in post-war Europe played a larger role in reconstruction than the World Bank. The World Bank loaned Western European countries $543 million from 1945–1950, while U.S. private investment was $1.76 billion for the same period. Therein lies the real success story of Europe's recovery. While it is true that funding from the World Bank, other financial institutions, and the Marshall Plan helped rebuild war-torn Europe, the biggest impact on Europe's economic recovery came from private foreign investment.

By the late 1950s, it became clear that the World Bank

had served its purpose. Europe and Japan were well on their way to recovering from World War II. Private foreign investment was pouring into these regions to take advantage of their renewed economic strength. America realized its economic dominance in the world as U.S. investment flowed abroad to fuel economic development and growth. At this time, the Bank faced a fundamental choice: It could dissolve because its major goal had been met, or it could evolve into something not imagined by its creators.

The World Bank's Transformation

Eventually, the World Bank decided on the second course. By the mid-1960s, the Bank began to transform itself from a lender of last resort to an international welfare agency to assist the poor and less developed countries of the world. In 1960, for example, the Bank created the International Development Agency (IDA), which makes subsidized loans to poor countries either unable to afford private commercial loans or regarded as bad credit risks. Even though the original mission statement made casual reference to the "less developed" world, the Bank's founders largely had envisioned this as purely advisory. Yet the Bank began to give more than advice to less developed countries; in the 1960s, it began to give them substantial loans.

The mastermind of this transformation was former U.S. Secretary of Defense Robert S. McNamara, who took charge of the World Bank in 1968. To fund McNamara's new international welfare clearinghouse, the Bank had to seek ever-increasing levels of contributions from donor countries.

Also under McNamara's watch, the Bank formulated a new concept, called "sustainable development," that became the IDA's principal mission. Stated simply, this means that less developed countries can achieve sustainable levels of economic development only if enough resources are transferred from wealthy countries to poor countries. If loans are any measure of success, McNamara was "successful" indeed. By 1981, when McNamara resigned as president of the World Bank, lending had grown more than tenfold, from $883 million to $12 billion. World Bank lending and grants continue to grow, today totaling over $20 billion.

The World Bank remains fully committed to this kind of thinking, with most of its bureaucrats dedicated to the McNamara dogma. A book published in 1995 by the World Bank and the International Monetary Fund to commemorate their 50-year anniversary claims that "This institutional evolution has been matched by a changing approach to development. The early focus on discrete projects has evolved into a broader emphasis on policies, strategies, and institutions, and a more holistic approach to development. . . . [The World Bank] Group's primary concern is to help borrowers reduce poverty and improve living standards by promoting sustainable growth and investment in people." In other words, the World Bank is not the institution created in 1944 by the Bretton Woods Agreement; it has changed from lender of last resort to international welfare agency.

Decades of Failed Policies

While many of the Bank's economists are free to acknowledge the importance of macroeconomic reform in the recipe for economic growth, many of the Bank's officials continue to place too much emphasis on the importance of multilateral institutions to less developed countries. For example, former World Bank President Lewis T. Preston said in 1995: "Of fundamental importance, the Bank Group has evolved from being simply a financier of development to being also a trusted advisor on development, sharing its global experience of what does and does not work and helping its member countries to apply the lessons. . . . Fifty years of experience have validated the Bank Group's fundamental objective today: helping borrowers reduce poverty and improve living standards through sustainable growth and investment in people."

Thus, the Bank seems to claim not only that it has been successful at reducing poverty and improving living standards in less developed countries, but also that its continued existence is vital to the economic prospects of less developed countries in the future. Yet all the evidence shows that this is not true. Since its inception, the World Bank has provided over $356 billion to countries around the world, mostly to the less developed world. But most recipients are no better off today than they were before receiving such aid. In fact,

World Bank Loans and Economic Growth

	First Year Receiving Loans	Total World Bank Loans Through 6/30/95 Millions US dollars	Total World Bank Loans per Capita Through 6/30/95	GDP per Capita, First Year Receiving Loans 1987 US dollars	GDP per Capita, 1992 1987 US dollars	Change in GDP per Capita, First Year -1992 1987 US dollars	Change in GDP per Capita, First Year -1992
Madagascar	1967	$1,270.8	$103	$333	$217	–$116	–35%
Malawi	1967	1,533.9	169	133	145	12	9%
Malaysia	1965	3,446.6	185	846	2600	1,754	207%
Mali	1968	979.9	109	202	246	44	22%
Mauritania	1965	539.0	259	516	476	–40	–8%
Morocco	1965	7,198.1	275	500	854	354	71%
Myanmar	1965	837.4	19	210	250	40	19%
Nepal	1970	1,394.1	70	143	178	35	25%
Nicaragua	1965	637.3	164	1752	875	–876	–50%
Niger	1965	589.3	72	605	280	–325	–54%
Nigeria	1965	7,151.1	70	351	360	9	3%
Pakistan	1965	10,289.8	86	183	375	192	105%
Panama	1965	901.3	358	1345	2231	886	66%
Papua New Guinea	1969	655.2	162	810	916	106	13%

Notes: This table lists some of the countries receiving World Bank loans between 1965 and 1970. This time window was chosen for several reasons: 1. To exclude the European countries who used the loans for reconstruction, 2. To ensure that the developing countries received their loans after independence, and 3. To allow a large enough time frame for development loans to influence the countries' development. All Organization for Economic Cooperation and Development (OECD) countries were excluded from this list. In addition, this table does not include the following loan recipients: China, Cyprus, Iran, Jordan, Liberia, Syria, and Uganda because reliable GDP data from 1965 to 1970 was unavailable. **Total World Bank Loans** includes all loans distributed to the listed countries by the International Bank for Reconstruction and Development and the International Development Association since the Bank's founding. **Total World Banks Loans per Capita:** The per capita figures are understated. Total World Bank Loans were divided by the 1992 population of the recipient countries, while most of the countries received the bulk of their loans in the 1960s and 1970s when their populations were smaller.

Sources: *World Data 1994* on CD-ROM and *World Tables 1987, 1995*, The World Bank.

many are worse off. Consider the following:

• Of the 66 less developed countries receiving money from the World Bank for more than 25 years (most for at least 30 years), 37 are no better off today than they were before they received such loans;

• Of these 37 countries, 20 actually are worse off today than they were before receiving aid from the World Bank;

• Of these 20, eight have economies that have shrunk by at least 20 percent since their first World Bank loan; and

• The remaining 17 countries have economies today that are essentially the same as when they first received aid from the World Bank.

While many countries are no better off today than before they received money from the World Bank, some have performed particularly poorly.

• From 1965 to 1995, Nicaragua received over $637 million in World Bank aid. Its per capita gross domestic product in 1965, measured in constant 1987 U.S. dollars, was $1,752. Today it is only $875, some 50 percent less than before Nicaragua received any aid.

• The African country of Niger received over $589 million in World Bank aid from 1965 to 1995. Yet its per capita Gross Domestic Product (GDP) has shrunk by 54 percent, from $605 in 1965 to $280 [in 1996].

The evidence shows that the World Bank has a poor track record. One might expect that at least half of its recipients would be better off economically today then before they started receiving such aid, but this is not the case. Many are actually worse off. After nearly three decades, it seems clear that most long-term recipients of World Bank loans still are not achieving "sustainable development."

Why World Bank Programs Fail

The main reason for a lack of economic growth in these countries is a corresponding lack of economic freedom. A lack of economic freedom prevents countries from creating wealth and prosperity, and a worldwide survey of economic freedom finds that many World Bank recipients have economies that are mostly not free or repressed. *The 1996 Index of Economic Freedom*, published by The Heritage Foundation, analyzes the level of economic freedom in 142 countries. The study considers ten economic factors—trade, taxation, government consumption, monetary policy, banking, foreign investment, wage and price controls, private property rights, regulation, and black markets—and categorizes each country as having a "free," "mostly free," "mostly not free," or "repressed" economy. The findings of the study demonstrate that a majority of World Bank loan and grant recipients do not have significant levels of economic freedom:

• Of the 60 long-term recipients of World Bank aid that were graded in *The 1996 Index of Economic Freedom*, 37 have economies that are "mostly not free" or "repressed."

• Only 23 long-term recipients of World Bank aid have economies that are "mostly free," and none have economies that are "free."

Thus, most long-term recipients of World Bank loans and grants still do not have significant levels of economic freedom. Moreover, those recipients that have performed particularly poorly are the least economically free:

• Of the 18 countries whose economies have shrunk since they have been World Bank recipients, 16 have either "mostly not free" or "repressed" economies.

Economic prosperity is not forthcoming in these countries because they do not have economic freedom. Rather, most have high taxes, barriers to trade, restrictions on foreign investment, banking systems in disarray, onerous government regulations, bad monetary policies, extensive wage and price controls, and large black markets. To be sure, 23 long-term recipients of World Bank aid do have mostly free economies, but most of these are in Latin America, an area which has benefited from several years of economic reform. Thus, their categorization as having mostly free economies is a recent phenomenon. It is good that they are making progress, but given the evidence elsewhere in the world, it would be difficult to attribute this progress to help from the World Bank.

Periodical Bibliography

The following articles have been selected to supplement the diverse views presented in this chapter. Addresses are provided for periodicals not indexed in the *Readers' Guide to Periodical Literature*, the *Alternative Press Index*, the *Social Sciences Index*, or the *Index to Legal Periodicals and Books*.

Scott Ainslie	"The Global Market Gives People Options," *A Common Place*, July 1996. Available from 21 S. 12th St., PO Box 500, Akron, PA 17501-0500.
George B.N. Ayittey	"African Thugs Keep Their Continent Poor," *Wall Street Journal*, January 2, 1998.
Leonardo Boff	"Global Challenge," *Index on Censorship*, Vol. 28, No. 1, January/February 1999.
Asad Ismi	"The World Bank: Sustainable Under-development," *Democratic Left*, Spring 1998.
Hal Kane	"Vital Signs: Income Gap Widens," *World Watch*, March/April 1996. Available from 1776 Massachusetts Ave. NW, Washington, DC 20036.
Jay Mandle	"The Good Side of Going Global," *Commonweal*, July 18, 1997.
Jay Mandle	"The Left's Wrong Turn," *Dissent*, Spring 1998.
Anna Manzo	"Rethinking Colonialism," *Toward Freedom*, November 1998. Available from 150 Cherry St. #3, Burlington, VT 05401.
Rashmi Mayur and Bennett Daviss	"How NOT to Develop an Emerging Nation," *Futurist*, January/February 1998.
Patrick McCormick	"Forgive Us Our Debts," *U.S. Catholic*, November 1998.
David Nicholson-Lord	"The Politics of Travel: Is Tourism Just Colonialism in Another Guise?" *Nation*, October 6, 1997.
Jeffrey D. Sachs	"A Millennial Gift to Developing Nations," *New York Times*, June 11, 1999.
Franz Schurmann	"Africa Is Saving Itself," *Choices*, June 1996. Available from the Division of Public Affairs, United Nations Development Programme, One United Nations Plaza, New York, NY 10017.
Ken Wells	"Economies of Scale: Microcredit Arrives in Africa, but Can It Match Asian Success?" *Wall Street Journal*, September 29, 1998.

CHAPTER 3

Can Third World Nations Form Lasting Democracies?

Chapter Preface

Democracies often have violent beginnings, because a government that has held power for many years is unlikely to expand political freedoms unless compelled by a rebelling populace. The transformation of Indonesia in the late 1990s from an autocracy into the world's third-largest democracy (behind the United States and India) is a modern illustration of this thesis.

The Indonesian revolution followed more than three decades of rule by President Suharto. His reign saw Indonesia make great economic strides. However, Indonesia's prosperity was coupled with newspaper censorship and other restrictions on political freedom.

Indonesia's economic success did not last, however, and the collapse of the nation's economy in the late 1990s led to the end of Suharto's reign. In spring 1998, protests over Suharto's inability to solve Indonesia's worst economic crisis in thirty years resulted in more than five hundred deaths. Demands by protesters that Suharto be removed from office came to fruition when he resigned on May 21, 1998. According to columnist James O. Goldsborough, Suharto saw his rule end ignominiously because "he committed a common (and always fatal) mistake among despots: He believed the nation . . . would accept higher standards of living without democracy."

B.J. Habibie, Suharto's successor and former vice president, began the process of democratization, initiating reforms that led to the founding of 140 political parties and greater freedom of speech and assembly. He also ended Indonesia's history of autocratic rule by calling for elections. On June 7, 1999, Indonesia held its first free election since 1955. Megawati Sukarnoputri (the daughter of Indonesia's founding president Sukarno) defeated Habibie, garnering 33.7 percent of the votes. As it turned out, when the Indonesian national assembly made its official decision, neither candidate was named president. Habibie withdrew his candidacy hours before the assembly's vote on October 20, 1999. Megawati lost the election to Muslim cleric Abdurrahman Wahid, but she was elected vice-president the following day.

Indonesia is just one Third World nation struggling to establish a democracy. In the following chapter, the authors debate whether developing nations can form lasting democracies.

1

> "The founders of [the Swiss] confederation
> were faced with problems similar to those
> of many of the present new democracies."

Imposing American-Style Democracy on Third World Nations May Be Harmful

James L. Tyson

In the following viewpoint, James L. Tyson asserts that de-veloping nations will have greater success at establishing lasting democracies if they adopt Switzerland's democratic model—a confederation of states. Tyson maintains that the confederation model—which gives more power to the can-tons (states) than to the federal government—is preferable to the Anglo-American structure for countries that lack a dom-inant religion or language. According to Tyson, if Third World nations adopted the Anglo-American model of na-tional parties and a powerful chief executive, a single politi-cal party could gain too much power. Tyson is the president of the Council for the Defense of Freedom, which seeks to combat Communist aggression and protect national security.

As you read, consider the following questions:
1. According to the author, what is the main structure in the history of Middle Eastern nations?
2. What does Tyson say would have happened if Switzerland had adopted the Anglo-American system?
3. In Tyson's opinion, what is one reason for Switzerland's success?

Excerpted from "Alternative Democracy: The American and British Model May Not Be the Best for All Emerging Nations," by James L. Tyson. This article appeared in the December 1996 issue of, and is reprinted with permission from, *The World & I*, a publication of The Washington Times Corporation, copyright ©1996.

The years since World War II have seen a tremendous flowering of new nation-states, colonies given their independence by the former colonial powers and, more recently, the countries emerging from the rubble of the Soviet bloc. Throughout this period, the United States has led the great powers in promoting "democracy" in these newly independent nations. But in the majority of cases, the results have been vastly disappointing. In almost every country, democracy has failed to take hold effectively. Throughout the former Soviet areas, among the Arab countries of the Middle East, across Africa, and in India and Southeast Asia, the disappearance of the colonial or communist regimes has usually been followed by great troubles, ranging from simple confusion to bloody chaos.

There are many reasons for the failure of democracy to take hold in these new nations, including racial, tribal, or religious tensions and the lack of experience and knowledge about the workings of democracy and self-government. But a few observers in the democracies and some citizens of the emerging nations themselves have been zeroing in on one major reason for many of the problems: that the Anglo-American model of democracy recommended for these new nations may in fact be quite inappropriate for their special political situations. Some commentators are now saying that many such countries should not attempt to use this model but something more like the Swiss confederation structure.

In view of the high percentage of failures, it is time to give more consideration to a study of the reasons for this. Because the promotion of democracy has become a major element of American foreign policy, we must research how it might be better implemented in the future.

Postwar Policies

In the postwar years, when it became evident that we were in a worldwide struggle with the Soviets for the minds of men around the world, a major campaign began with the revival of the wartime U.S. Information Agency and the Voice of America and the launching of two new services, Radio Free Europe and Radio Liberty.

After the collapse of the Soviet bloc, our missionary efforts became even more explicit. George Bush declared after the fall of the Berlin Wall and the collapse of the Soviet Union that we were entering a "New World Order." During Secretary of State James Baker's shuttle diplomacy in the Middle East, he stated that he was attempting to promote democracy as well as peace in that region.

The same has continued under the Clinton administration. [Former secretary of state] Warren Christopher has said that his efforts in the Middle East have been aimed at promoting democracy as well as the difficult problem of an Arab-Israeli settlement. The statement by then Secretary of Defense Les Aspin on March 27, 1993, releasing the administration's defense budget, declared that "the spread of democracy around the world supports U.S. security and fosters global stability and prosperity that can benefit all peoples. . . . The Clinton administration will act vigorously to promote democratic reforms."

So if this effort continues to be a major part of the American foreign-policy agenda, it is important that we examine why it has met with so much failure up to now and what better policies might be followed in the future.

Defining the Anglo-American Model

A good starting point is to define the characteristics of the Anglo-American model, why it is unsuitable for many new nations, and what the alternatives are. Aside from a few differences between the American and British systems, the main common characteristics are the following:

- nationwide political parties;
- periodic nationwide elections for a legislature and chief executive;
- a national legislature in which the majority party or coalition wields great power; and
- a chief executive also wielding large powers over the executive functions.

What some commentators in Europe like to call the "Anglo-Saxon model" is fairly satisfactory for a nation that has a certain degree of homogeneity. In the United States and Britain, we generally speak the same language, and our religious beliefs, while not identical, at least do not usually lead to violent conflicts. In the United States and Britain, those minorities that are different in color, race, language, or religion have experienced various forms of discrimination, but these are being gradually addressed. Despite such problems as the religious violence in Northern Ireland and the troubles of urban blacks in the United States, most conflicts today are not serious enough to rend the fabric of the nation as a whole.

France, Italy, and the other relatively homogeneous west European democracies have also installed this system with a fair degree of success.

Political Problems in Developing Countries

But in many new post–World War II nations the situation is vastly different. The Arab countries of the Middle East are extreme examples. Following World War I and the collapse of the Ottoman Empire, the Middle Eastern areas of the empire were divided up by the victorious British and French. Their statesmen took a map of the area and literally using rulers created polygons with straight borders and sharp angles that had little relation to the tribal loyalties or even the physical terrain but were only designed to satisfy the needs of the victors. Thus Syria, Lebanon, Iraq, Trans-Jordan, Palestine, and the Yemens were created and became "protectorates" with little regard for the history or desires of the inhabitants. Following World War II these countries were given their independence and joined the ranks of new nation-states.

In most of these countries, however, there was little experience of or sympathy for the idea of a nation-state. The main structure in their history has been the tribe, a vital institution in maintaining the loyalty and security of individuals in the difficult nomadic, herding culture of the region. First loyalties usually are to the family, then the tribe, and perhaps further to a coalition of tribes.

There are also important religious splits in these countries. In Lebanon there are many Christians as well as the two major Muslim sects, the Sunnis and Shiites, and the Druse, an offshoot of Islam. In Syria there are the Sunnis and another important fanatical Muslim sect called the Alawites. In Iraq there are large populations of both Sunnis and Shiites, which have traditionally mistrusted each other, as well as large numbers of Kurds.

In turning over these nations to their inhabitants, the European democracies attempted to pass on all the trappings of Western democratic states: nationwide political parties, a parliament, the office of president, and even a national anthem and a flag. But the results have been tragic. In Syria, Iraq, Yemen, and Libya it has been a matter of which tribal leader can fight his way to the top by ruthless means. Thus, we now see such tyrants as Saddam Hussein and Hafez Assad in power. Lebanon had many years of peace and prosperity under a complicated agreement for sharing authority among its three major groups, but this eventually collapsed in the face of intrigue and aggression by its ruthless neighbors. So the region continues to be characterized by tension and almost continuous violence.

In Trans-Jordan, Saudi Arabia, the Gulf Emirates, and most North African Arab states there has been more stability, either because of more homogeneity or because the ruling monarchs are less brutal and authoritarian.

For the problem states of Syria, Lebanon, Iraq, Yemen, and Libya, the Swiss confederation model by itself may not be the miracle road to peace and freedom. Certainly one important first step would be to allow a complete revision of borders and political authorities more in line with tribal realities. But then the confederation model would certainly be another step to bring about structures that would make it less likely that one tribe, usually the most unscrupulous, would be able to dominate all the others, as under the present artificial nationwide parliaments and presidencies.

The Swiss Model

The confederation form of democracy has already been successfully employed for more than a century in Switzerland, a clear example of a country with religious and language differences that would make the Anglo-American model almost intolerable.

Many of the Swiss states, or cantons, are the oldest democracies still in operation in the world. Originally they were small independent identities, some of which had been making democracy work at the local level for centuries, with long traditions of religious and political toleration, allowing them to be havens for controversial figures like Voltaire, Rousseau, Zwingli, Calvin, and others (including Lenin and his followers). Three of these cantons formed their first alliance in 1291. The alliance grew, and after a period of French occupation following 1798, they gained their independence again in 1815. In 1848 they drew up their first federal constitution.

The Historical Basis of African Confederalism

Most of the countries in Africa are linguistically, politically, and ethnically diverse. In addition, colonial occupation introduced Africans to many foreign institutions, such as European languages and cultures, private property rights, the exchange economy, Christianity, and Islam. These institutions have had a significant impact on pluralism in the continent and may need to be considered when determining the optimal number of political units for each country.

Several authors have made a compelling case for a return to *confederalism*, which existed in many pre-colonial African societies (e.g., the great empires of Ghana, Mali, and Great Zimbabwe). This was characterized by significant decentralization and devolution of authority to local political jurisdictions. Confederalism provided the structures for the peaceful coexistence of the various ethnic groups in Africa. Thus, some scholars have suggested that in the present transition the continent refrain from relying on European or other imported institutional models and instead return to Africa's indigenous institutions.

John Mukum Mbaku, *Independent Review*, Spring 1998.

The founders of this confederation were faced with problems similar to those of many of the present new democracies. The population was divided into three language groups: German, French, and Italian (and even a fourth, lesser-known language: Romansh). If they had adopted the Anglo-American system—with national parties, nationwide elections, a national legislature, and a powerful chief executive—then one language group, almost certainly the Germans, would have won the majority in Parliament, elected the chief executive, and wielded power that would have been intolerable to the other communities.

Instead they developed the federal cantonal system, with many functions reserved for the cantons and with the powers of the central executive limited to certain essentials like foreign affairs, security, international trade and finance, and so forth.

There are twenty-two cantons, each with its own constitution. The cantons elect representatives to a bicameral national legislature every four years. The legislature then elects the cabinet (Bundesrat) of only seven members for four-year terms. These officials head the seven administrative departments of the federal government. Each year the legislature elects one member of the cabinet to be president for a one-year term only. He has little more power than other members of the cabinet and cannot be reelected until he has been out of office at least a year.

The result of this structure has been that the four language communities have lived in peace and prosperity for more than a century, with one of the most stable societies (and currencies) in the world. . . .

The Dangers of the Anglo-American Model

Many . . . nations have . . . problems with racial, language, and religious rivalries, which cause great difficulties if the Anglo-American model is adopted. A dramatic description of such problems was given in October 1982 at one of the U.S. State Department conferences on "Democratization in Communist Countries." The State Department sponsored several such meetings as part of the Reagan administration's efforts to promote democracy, in line with the president's speech before the British Parliament in June of that year.

This particular conference was addressed by several American and foreign experts on political science from academia, the government, and private think tanks. After an opening address by [then-Secretary of State] George Shultz, the talks ranged over the possibilities and methods for promoting democracy in communist-dominated and other authoritarian countries. But one representative of a Third World nation, who insisted on remaining anonymous in the published transcripts, said that none of the speakers up until then had mentioned the problem that the American system of national parties and one all-powerful chief executive might be disastrous for his and many other Third World nations. He said it could be literally a "matter of life or death" for him and many other leaders. If one party in his country were allowed to take total power, he and some of his associates might be executed. He added that in countries with bitter tribal or language differences, some form of federal system was absolutely essential.

The Swiss confederation model, of course, is not a miracle cure for all Third World problems. Even its proponents grant that it is not an ideal form of government, or the most effective in promoting quick and decisive action on all governmental problems. But it is undoubtedly preferable to the Anglo-American model for nations with mixed populations.

Some of Switzerland's success is due to the fact that it has been able to preserve its neutrality within its Alpine strongholds while much of the rest of the world has been torn by wars and revolutions. The system was undoubtedly the preferable one for Switzerland and other nations with similar racial or religious differences.

As Winston Churchill said, "Democracy is a very poor form of government. The problem is that all the other forms are so much worse." A confederation is not an ideal structure for ensuring an efficient administration, as our Founding Fathers discovered before drawing up our Constitution. But the problem is that all the other forms, including the Anglo-American model, are so much worse for many countries.

> *"The clear-sightedness of [Nigeria and*
> *South Africa's] leaders have demonstrated*
> *to the world that Africans are more than*
> *capable of meeting the demands of*
> *democracy."*

Democracy Can Succeed in Africa

Amii Omara-Otunnu

The 1999 elections in Nigeria and South Africa indicate that democracy can be sustained in Africa, argues Amii Omara-Otunnu in the following viewpoint. According to Omara-Otunnu, the actions of Nigerian president Olusegun Obasanjo, South Africa's former president Nelson Mandela, and Mandela's successor Thabo Mbeki are proof that democratic governments in Africa can fight corruption and better their citizens' lives. In addition, he maintains that the West must provide economic and diplomatic support to these nations and cease aiding nondemocratic leaders, in order to ensure that democracy can thrive throughout Africa. Omara-Otunnu is a history professor at the University of Connecticut in Storrs.

As you read, consider the following questions:
1. What actions did Obasanjo take upon entering office, as stated by the author?
2. According to statistics cited by Omara-Otunnu, what percentage of South Africans voted in the 1999 election?
3. Why are Nigeria and South Africa barometers for the rest of Africa, in the author's view?

Excerpted from "Democracy Burns Bright in Africa," by Amii Omara-Otunnu, *Newsday*, June 16, 1999. Reprinted with the permission of Amii Omara-Otunnu.

From Africa, where scarcely any good news is reported, has come an inspiring, trend-setting change in the two most strategic African countries, Nigeria and South Africa. The omens are good that they will help redeem the promise of a continent that has been obscured by the maelstrom of dictatorships and civil wars in the past three decades. The West must not fail them.

A Watershed Political Moment

Within the past few weeks [in late May 1999 and early June 1999], the elections in Nigeria and South Africa have marked a watershed in African political history. In both countries, the extraordinary political courage of the people and the clear-sightedness of their leaders have demonstrated to the world that Africans are more than capable of meeting the demands of democracy.

In Nigeria, Olusegun Obasanjo, the first democratically elected civilian president in 15 years, set the tone for his administration when he vowed during his inauguration that he will tackle head-on the pervasive corruption that has crippled the country. Within a week, he sent powerful signals about his seriousness when he appointed two independent commissions, one charged with responsibility to review governmental contracts awarded by the past military regime and find out whether they were awarded properly and for bona fide purposes; the other mandated to investigate all cases of human rights violations that have occurred in the past 15 years, beginning with the regime of the vicious military dictator, Gen. Sani Abacha. These decisive actions by Obasanjo, in a country like Nigeria where political leaders have scarcely ever questioned the action of the military establishment, must be applauded as courageous.

In South Africa, the people defied the gloom-and-doom soothsayers who had forecast that the second democratic election since the end of apartheid would be marred by violence and characterized by apathy. In an impressive exercise of democratic rights, South Africans rose like a tidal wave, as 85 percent of the electorate voted in an almost violence-free election. The remarkably high turnout is a valuable lesson not only for Africa but the entire world. The example set by the people has been matched by the pledge of Nelson Mandela's successor, Thabo Mbeki, that his administration will focus on tackling the problems of economic inequality and poverty, unemployment and escalating crime.

Mandela's Legacy

If Mbeki can deliver on his promise, it will crown the already enviable record of the African National Congress. Since coming to power five years ago, the ANC, led by Mandela, has provided clean piped water to 3 million people and housing and telephones to another 3 million people, and has brought into the school system for the first time 1.5 million more children.

Mandela himself has set an admirable example for other leaders by serving only one five-year term. With his charisma

The Quality of Life in South Africa

Delivery of Services

% of Households With:	1994	1998–99
Electricity	31%	63%
Water	30%	44%
Telephones	25%	35%
TV reception (a)	70%	85%

Demographics

	1994	1998–99
Population, in millions	38.6	40.6 (b)
Life expectancy, in years	62.7 (c)	65.0 (b)
Infant mortality, per 1,000 live births	40.2 (d)	36.0 (b)
Unemployment rate	29.2%	37.6% (e)
Murder rate, per 100,000 people	69.3	58.5
GDP per capita, in U.S. dollars	$3,076	$2,695

Notes: (a) Based on total population, not households; (b) Based on 1996 census; (c) Based on 1991 data; (d) Based on 1990 data; (e) Based on 1997 data.

Government Communication & Information System; Statistics South Africa; South African Police Service; South African Revenue Service; Department of Health and Welfare.

and huge popularity among all races in South Africa, a lesser leader than Mandela could very easily have decided to remain in power. But in a remarkable testimony to his moral character, Mandela—like George Washington many years ago, in a decision that has had an enormous impact on U.S. constitutional development—left office before power and the phenomenon of hero worship could corrupt him. Those who care about the future of Africa hope that other African leaders will learn from him and follow suit.

What happens in these two countries has been, and will be, a barometer for the rest of Africa for three main reasons. First, Nigeria and South Africa are the undisputed military and economic powers in Africa. Second, Nigeria is the most populous country in the continent. With a population of about 120 million people, one in four Africans lives in that country. And third, there is a considerable reservoir of good will for South Africa in its attempts to build a nonracial society.

The good will is a holdover from the moral and political resources that progressive and black people all over the world invested in the overthrow of apartheid. Any success in South Africa would not only serve as a model of race relations for the rest of the world but would also be a fitting reward for those who struggled in solidarity with the majority of South Africans to dismantle the institutionalized racism of the apartheid system.

Nigeria and South Africa Must Stay Strong

For Africa's prospects in the new millennium, it is imperative that these two key countries not falter. Although the policies being pursued by Obasanjo in Nigeria and Mbeki in South Africa have begun to inspire and uplift the spirit of ordinary people in both countries, they may not be sufficient to yield sustainable economic and social development. The international community and the West in particular should provide additional diplomatic and financial support to both countries to consolidate the initial success. But equally important, the West needs to cease giving dispensation to antidemocratic rulers, such as Yoweri Museveni of Uganda and Paul Kagame of Rwanda, who still retain the discredited dogma of a one-party state, combined with faith in militarism. Any support by the West for client rulers who do not subscribe to the principles of democratic pluralism only undermines efforts for democratic renewal in South Africa, Nigeria and elsewhere.

Nigeria's and South Africa's democratically elected leaders have begun their mission to keep hope alive. The early policy pronouncements by both Thabo Mbeki of South Africa and Olusegun Obasanjo of Nigeria have sounded a clarion call.

They can chart the right course not only for their respective countries but for the continent as a whole. With these two powerful countries anchoring democratic pluralism, Africa will claim its rightful place in the world. That is a good tiding from Africa, and it is of global significance.

| "If democracy is about throwing the rascals out, then it is not working in Africa."

Problems Persist in African Democracies

The Economist

In the following viewpoint, *The Economist*, an authoritative British publication, asserts that democracy in Africa has been unsuccessful because elections have largely failed to produce a change in government. The ruling parties use their power to manipulate elections, the magazine contends. According to *The Economist*, African nations may need to consider their past political structures in order to develop democratically.

As you read, consider the following questions:
1. In the magazine's view, what does voting for the African National Congress express?
2. According to statistics cited by *The Economist*, how many of the elections held by forty-two sub-Saharan African countries resulted in a change of government?
3. How could some elections have been won, in *The Economist*'s opinion?

Within a week [in late May and early June 1999], the two most important countries in sub-Saharan Africa, South Africa and Nigeria, have gone through a solemn democratic ritual. South Africa held its second multi-racial general election on June 2, 1999. In Nigeria, 16 years of military rule came to an end when the generals handed over power to an elected president on May 29, 1999. Both occasions are joyful. But, at the same time, both South Africa and Nigeria demonstrate the immense difficulties that democracy is encountering in Africa. . . .

Unchanged Governments

The suspense [in South Africa], such as it was, was not whether the ruling African National Congress (ANC) would win, but how overwhelmingly it would win: the big question was whether it would get a two-thirds majority and thus theoretically be able to change the constitution. If the party hangs together, there is no foreseeable prospect of a change of government through elections. The party still wears the cloak of a liberation movement and, as such, it is more than a political party for black South Africans. Voting for it is an expression of ethnic or personal solidarity, not support for a set of principles or policies. That is the way it works in Africa. [The ANC fell one seat short of a two-thirds majority.]

Nigeria, despite the formal change of government, will still be largely run by its corrupt elite. It will take a long time to curb the power of their money, even if Olusegun Obasanjo, Nigeria's new ruler, tries to take them on. It was the well-connected "big men" who bankrolled the political parties, chose the leaders and paid people to vote for them. The lawyers and human-rights activists who had campaigned bravely for democracy during the years of military dictatorship were nowhere to be seen. During the campaign there was no debate on issues.

If democracy is about throwing the rascals out, then it is not working in Africa. At the end of the 1980s, Africa was hit by the democratic revolution sweeping Europe. Under internal and external pressure, dictators were forced to dismantle their one-party states and hold elections. Until that time, there had been only four functioning multi-party democracies in Africa: Botswana, Senegal, Gambia and Mauritius. And the first three of these never managed to produce a change of government.

Election Manipulation

With three decades of melding party and state structures to the point of being indistinguishable, incumbent leaders dedicated all their resources to ensuring that the opposition had very little chance of emerging victorious while maintaining, sometimes unsuccessfully, a facade of a free and fair balloting. Actual tactics differed from country to country, as did the degree to which incumbents bent the rules. In Tanzania, opposition politicians were denied sufficient access to the state-controlled mass media, which significantly reduced their ability to reach the vast majority of the rural population. In neighboring Kenya, President Moi ensured that the playing field remained unequal by refusing to license opposition party rallies and by harassing opposition activists. At the same time, poorly structured electoral reform meant that Moi was able to claim a new mandate despite having received only about 33 percent of the vote—no legal provisions for runoff elections existed. Others were less subtle in their approach. Equatorial Guinea's military strongman Colonel Teodoro Mbasogo required that voters fill in their ballots in full view of government officials. Mbasogo's election strategy also included having his main rival arrested and sentenced to death by a military tribunal, a sentence that was commuted to exile by Mbasogo upon his election victory.

James Mwangi and Kaniaru Wacieni, *Harvard International Review*, Spring 1997.

During the 1990s, a further 42 sub-Saharan African countries (out of 50), all of them either one-party states or military dictatorships, have held elections of varying credibility. In only ten of these was the government changed. And when it came to the election after that, in only two countries— Madagascar and Benin—did the voters throw out the elected government. Whom did they vote for instead? Astonishingly, they both plumped for the military men who had been deposed to make way for democracy. The only other African country where a democratically elected government has been turned out in an election is Mauritius which, like Madagascar, is an Indian Ocean island and African by location rather than culture. In Africa, the incumbents, however bad, tend to win elections.

Incumbents Have Too Much Power

When the democratic wave broke over Africa, some called it "the second liberation". It was hoped that the continent, freed from tyranny, would at last begin to develop. But, so far, there seems little correlation between democracy and economic success. With disillusion has come the fear that elections neither can nor will change anything.

The ruling parties and their leaders manipulate the vote with ease. Most African heads of state see nothing odd in using the trappings of office to campaign for re-election. While an opposition leader has to depend on donated cars and advertise only when he can afford it, the head of state zips around in a government helicopter and uses his nightly slot on the radio and television news (many of which lead off, "His Excellency, President X, said yesterday . . .") to promote his electoral chances. Some presidents also appoint those who run the election. And, when all else fails, they can loot the treasury to buy votes.

With only a small middle class, many of whose members owe their wealth to their closeness to the government, opposition parties are poor and fractious, and defections to a cosy official job are common. In this way, the ruling lot find it easy to play one ethnic group off against another. Several elections could have been won by the opposition if it had managed to be more united.

There seems to be little thought given to alternative democratic systems more suited to African societies. Uganda is experimenting with a no-party-system, and Ethiopia insists on parties that are ethnically based. Certainly, both systems serve to maintain the existing regimes in power. At the same time, it can be argued that they are attempts to develop democratic ways that incorporate African realities. Africa should look to its past—when there were councils of elders and other counterweights to royal or chiefly power—for political structures that suit its society, say some. But there is little debate about how structures from the past could be incorporated into modern democracies.

*"Democracy must be deepened to transform
the narrow, elitist rule that has long
characterized Latin America."*

Latin American Countries Need to Overcome Their Non-Democratic Past

Thomas J. D'Agostino

Democratic consolidation (the process by which emerging democracies ensure their citizens' ability to participate in and be represented by the government) in Latin America will require overcoming several obstacles, Thomas J. D'Agostino maintains in the following viewpoint. He argues that government corruption, autonomous militaries, and a non-democratic past are key reasons why establishing strong and broad democracies has been difficult in Latin America. D'Agostino contends that Latin American political parties can help provide stability if the political and economic desires of their supporters are fulfilled. D'Agostino is an assistant professor of political science at Siena College in Loudonville, New York.

As you read, consider the following questions:

1. What has shaken popular support for democracy in Brazil and Venezuela, according to the author?
2. In D'Agostino's view, what has limited democracy in Caribbean nations?
3. What are some of the characteristics of Latin American political parties, as stated by the author?

Excerpted from "Latin American Politics," by Thomas J. D'Agostino, in *Understanding Contemporary Latin America*, ed. Richard S. Hillman. Copyright ©1997 by Lynne Rienner Publishers, Inc. Reprinted with the permission of Lynne Rienner Publishers Inc.

Although by the early 1990s there were signs of economic improvement in some countries [in Latin America], and a number of peaceful transfers of power had occurred, the fragility of democratic civilian rule was evident. In some cases, popular support for democratic leaders and institutions was severely undermined by deteriorating socioeconomic conditions and pervasive corruption and fraud, and elsewhere the region's strong authoritarian tradition and powerful opposition to democracy will be much more difficult to overcome in some countries than in others.

Threats to Democracy

In Haiti, for example, [President Jean Bertrand] Aristide was deposed just months into his term by military forces acting on behalf of the nation's small but powerful elite. Thousands were killed or fled the country in a wave of violence following the coup as the military and paramilitary "attachés" sought to rid Haiti of Aristide supporters. Only after intense pressure and the threat of a U.S. invasion did the military relent, allowing Aristide to return to Haiti to complete his term. In Peru, [President Alberto] Fujimori's frustration over his inability to implement reforms and to wage war against narcotraffickers and the Shining Path [a Peruvian revolutionary group, viewed by many as terrorists] led to an *autogolpe* (self-coup) in 1992 in which he suspended the constitution, closed the national congress, and began to rule by decree. Although strongly supported by a public tired of violence, this move toward "presidential authoritarianism" demonstrated a disdain for democratic institutions and principles that does not bode well for the future. A similar attempt by Guatemalan President Jorge Serrano to carry out an *autogolpe* was thwarted, although it provided further evidence of the vulnerability of democracy in some societies.

Widespread corruption—at times reaching the highest levels of government—and electoral fraud have plagued some political systems, diminishing faith not only in individual leaders but in democracy itself. In Mexico, it is widely held that the ruling PRI (Institutional Revolutionary Party) has rigged elections to maintain the monopoly on power it has held since 1929. Despite the pledge of recent PRI leaders to reform, opposition parties (as well as international observers) allege that elections ranging from the 1998 presidential contest to more recent state and local races have been marred by fraud. Similarly, the 1990 and 1994 presidential elections in the Dominican Republic, in which incumbent Joaquín Balaguer was narrowly reelected, were marred by allegations of fraud and the dubious performance of electoral institutions. In both cases, popular confidence in the institutions of democracy has been severely compromised.

In Brazil and Venezuela, popular support for democracy has been shaken by the removal of democratically elected presidents. Brazil's Fernando Collor de Mello, the country's first directly elected civilian leader since 1960, took office in 1990 pledging to fight corruption. By 1992, Collor de Mello had resigned from office after being impeached amid allegations of financial misconduct. Venezuela's long-standing democracy was challenged by two coup attempts against the government of Carlos Andrés Pérez in 1992. Popular opposition to Pérez, stemming from charges of corruption and the imposition of harsh austerity measures, had grown so great that the coup leaders were widely supported. Pérez was removed from office the following year, accused of misusing funds, and was later indicted to stand trial. In a country where economic decline has diminished support for traditional parties and civilian leaders, the demise of the Pérez government further undermined popular perceptions of democratic rule. Although the image of both the Brazilian and Venezuelan political systems was tarnished by these events, it is significant that in both instances democratic processes were employed successfully to remove the leaders.

The Prospects for Consolidation

For the current era of democratization to be sustained, some rather significant obstacles must be overcome. For example, elected civilian leaders throughout Latin America will have to deal with national military institutions that, despite generally inauspicious performances while in power, have traditionally enjoyed considerable autonomy (essentially comprising a "fourth branch" of government) and have played a very active political role. Democratic consolidation will require greater civilian control over the military, not an easy task given this traditional role. Moreover, civil-military relations have been tense in countries such as Argentina (where a number of barracks revolts have occurred since 1983), Chile (where General [Augusto] Pinochet remains head of the army), and El Salvador (where the issue of prosecuting those involved in human rights abuses has been volatile). Although few military leaders in the region are eager to return to power, the constitutional mandate to preserve order and stability raises the possibility of some form of military intervention if civilian leaders prove incapable of keeping the peace.

In many respects, Latin America will have to overcome its past to continue the process of democratic consolidation. Because of a persistently low level of institutionalization, many of the former Iberian colonies possess a relatively weak foundation on which to establish a stable, democratic political system. A variety of factors have impeded institutional development, including the tradition of personalism and the intense repression and demobilization practiced by bureaucratic authoritarian regimes.

Even in the Commonwealth Caribbean, where strong political institutions and democratic structures were imported through British colonialism, the prospects for further consolidation are mixed. The Westminster model of parliamentary democracy, "Caribbeanized" to fit the regional context, now exhibits strong authoritarian features. Elitism and limited mass participation, pervasive patron clientelism, and the dominance of personalistic leaders such as Vere Bird (Antigua), Eric Gairy (Grenada), Eric Williams (Trinidad), and Michael Manley (Jamaica) have limited democracy in practice. Moreover [according to professor Jean Grugel], in a region where "democracy has been shown to be stable primarily where it is related to the establishment of concrete material gains for most of the population," consolidation has been hindered by economic stagnation and declining living standards. Popular confidence in democratic leaders and institutions has diminished, leading to increased alienation and violence and threatening stability.

Strengthening Latin American democracy will require measures to curtail the powers of the executive while bolstering those of the legislature and the judiciary as autonomous branches of government. Further, democracy must be deepened to transform the narrow, elitist rule that has long characterized Latin America. This process may come about through the formation of a variety of organizations, including neighborhood associations and peasant groups, to give voice to popular demands. Such demands may also be channeled through political parties and party systems, widely recognized as the key to stable, democratic rule.

Evaluating Latin American Political Parties

The existence of formal democratic bodies, such as political parties and competitive elections, does not alone necessarily guarantee representative government. Parties and elections perform critical functions, however, and are essential components of democratic systems. In the past, elections represented only one of several means of gaining and legitimizing power. Nevertheless, although their importance has fluctuated considerably over time, much more attention has been devoted to competitive elections and party politics because of their recent resurgence after decades of repression under military rule.

Party politics in Latin America has its origin in the early postindependence era when informal elite groups coalesced into Conservative and Liberal parties. Other types of parties began to appear in the more socioeconomically advanced Southern Cone countries [Argentina, Chile, Bolivia, Peru, Paraguay, and Uruguay] during the late 1800s–early 1900s in response to the impact of modernization. The rise of an educated, politically aware middle class that sought access to the political process led to the formation of reformist parties, the most prominent being the Radical Civic Union in Argentina and the Colorado Party in Uruguay. As electorates diversified with industrialization, party systems expanded with the emergence of Marxist, nationalist-populist, and Christian Democratic organizations. In Jamaica and elsewhere in the British Caribbean, labor union activity during the tumultuous 1930s, coupled with the movement toward self-government, fostered the emergence of modern political party systems. The party-union bond was strong and represented "one pillar of the democratic order" in the Anglophone Caribbean at the time of independence.

Logically, there has been considerable diversity among Latin American parties in terms of ideological orientations, the structure of party systems, and the relative importance of parties in their respective systems. A significant degree of ideological variation has occurred in the past, ranging from Marxism to fascism, although parties have become increasingly pragmatic. Latin American party systems have ranged from vibrant multiparty systems to stable two-party arrangements to authoritarian one-party states to cases where no viable parties exist.

The Latin American Culture

Latin America's chronically poor policies and weak institutions—and what may appear as persistent poor judgment—are principally a cultural phenomenon flowing from the traditional Ibero-Catholic system of values and attitudes. That culture focuses on the present and the past at the expense of the future; it focuses on the individual and the family at the expense of the broader society; it nurtures authoritarianism; it propagates a flexible ethical code; it enshrines orthodoxy; and it is disdainful of work, creativity, and saving. It is that culture that chiefly explains why, as we approach the end of the twentieth century, Latin America lags so far behind the United States and Canada.

Lawrence E. Harrison, *The Pan-American Dream: Do Latin America's Cultural Values Discourage True Partnership with the United States and Canada?* 1997.

Such diversity notwithstanding, [Latin American political scholars] Ronald McDonald and J. Mark Ruhl recognized some important characteristics common to most Latin American parties. First, they tend to be elitist, in that those who wield power within the parties are drawn predominantly from the middle classes. Second, Latin American parties are often highly factionalized as a result of ideological, policy, or personal disputes. A third common characteristic is the dominance of individual leaders and the importance of personalism in politics. Parties are frequently organized around individual personalities, often serving merely as electoral vehicles for those aspiring to power. Such parties typically lack any significant programmatic or ideological base. Fourth, many Latin American parties possess a very weak organizational structure. Although some of the most notable parties in the region (Mexico's Partido Revolucionario Institucional/Institutional Revolutionary Party [PRI], Peru's American Popular Revolutionary Alliance [APRA], and Democratic Action [or Acción Democrática] [AD] in Venezuela) maintain an elaborate, permanent organizational apparatus, this has been the exception rather than the rule. It has been common for parties to appear around election time to support a particular individual and then to disappear when the leader passes from the scene. Finally, unlike Western European parties, which tend to be class-based, Latin American parties maintain a broad, heterogeneous base of support.

Another area of divergence between parties in Latin America and those found in Western Europe (or North America) lies in the nature of the functions they perform. European and U.S. parties function as recruiters of new members, aggregators and articulators of interests, developers of programs, and selectors of candidates to compete for office. Latin American parties, however, which do not necessarily carry out these tasks as envisioned, also serve a number of other purposes. For example, in authoritarian systems, such as Cuba under [Fidel] Castro and the Dominican Republic under Rafael Trujillo, parties were created as a means of mobilizing support for the regime and of maintaining social control. In the cases of Brazil during the military dictatorship (1964–1985) and Nicaragua during the Somoza dynasty, the existence of parties and elections was viewed as a method of legitimization. As noted earlier, many Latin American parties have served as electoral vehicles for personalistic leaders. Many also function predominantly as machines through which patronage and favors are dispensed in return for support. In this sense, party organizations have served to channel popular participation and, in the process, have facilitated the co-optation of the masses into the existing framework under elite tutelage.

The persistence of personalism and patron clientelism alongside increasingly complex organizational structures and campaign techniques reflects the blending of traditional and modern patterns. The continued dominance of personalistic leaders, however, has often impeded the institutionalization of parties and party systems. Nevertheless, party politics and elections have been revitalized during this era of democratization. Elections have become the exclusive legitimate means of gaining power, and parties, which are exhibiting a greater degree of organization and are articulating viable programs, appear to offer much potential for managing the destabilizing impact of modernization. Thus far, however, political parties and their leaders have been only partially effective in ameliorating endemic problems. As long as basic political and socioeconomic aspirations go unfulfilled, support for political parties will diminish, the legitimacy of democratic governments will be called into question, and the stability of many Latin American states will remain precarious.

Governments Need to Be Effective

The current transition toward democratic rule in Latin America has been bolstered by an international environment in which Western-style democracy and free-market capitalism have prevailed. Domestic conditions have been less fortuitous, however, and in much of Latin America democratic institutions and principles are not well rooted because of the lack of a long, successful democratic tradition and a corresponding "reservoir of legitimacy." Elected civilian leaders throughout the region, including Caribbean states in which democracy is perceived to be established and stable, are under great pressure, because their ability to maintain support through the use of patronage and clientelist links has been constrained by stagnant economies or the imposition of economic restructuring programs. Although democratic values are spreading and in theory democracy is enjoying widespread support, Latin American publics are increasingly pragmatic and demand quick solutions to their problems. Clearly, the key to consolidating democracy and averting a devolution to authoritarian rule is for governments to perform effectively. Democracy is very much on trial in Latin America, and the verdict will ultimately rest on the degree to which mass publics call be satisfied without unduly provoking elites.

5

"*The long-awaited democracies [in Latin America] have not fulfilled their role as guardians of public order.*"

Unchecked Power Threatens Latin American Democracies

Paulo Sérgio Pinheiro, translated by Judy Rein

In the following viewpoint, Paulo Sérgio Pinheiro claims that democracy in Latin America has failed because not all citizens are equally protected from violence. According to Pinheiro, the Latin American poor are victimized by common crime and by police who use violence to protect the rich against the poor. He asserts that Latin American democratic states need to end the repressive tactics of the police and military. Pinheiro is director of the Center for the Study of Violence at the University of São Paulo in Brazil and a member of the editorial board of the North American Congress on Latin America (NACLA), an independent nonprofit organization that provides information on major trends in Latin America and its relations with the United States.

As you read, consider the following questions:
1. According to Pinheiro, who are the primary targets of police violence in Brazil?
2. What is the murder rate for São Paulo residents between the ages of fifteen and twenty-four, according to statistics cited by the author?
3. In Pinheiro's view, what is the purpose of Latin American crime-prevention policies?

Excerpted from "Democracies Without Citizenship," by Paulo Sérgio Pinheiro, tran. Judy Rein, *NACLA Report on the Americas*, vol. 30, no. 2, pp. 17–24, September/October 1996. Copyright ©1997 by the North American Congress on Latin America. Reprinted with the permission of NACLA (475 Riverside Drive #454, New York, NY 10115-0122).

I n Brazil, as in many Latin American countries, there is a dramatic gap between the letter of the law and the brutal reality of law enforcement. Brazil's new Constitution, promulgated in 1988, incorporated broad provisions for the protection of individual rights, which were systematically violated during two decades of military rule. The document explicitly recognizes the rights to life, liberty and personal integrity, and torture and racial discrimination are now considered crimes. But despite these constitutional protections, official violence continues unabated.

This gap between the law and reality is rooted in the failure of Latin American democracies to consolidate one of the most basic cornerstones of democratic governance: the state's monopoly over the means of coercion. This failure has resulted in the persistence of endemic violence throughout the region. On the one hand, violence is exercised by elites to maintain "social order." In countries like Brazil, deadly force, torture and arbitrary detention continue to characterize police behavior because this official violence enjoys widespread impunity. On the other hand, violent crime and delinquency have also increased in Latin American societies, particularly in the 1980s and 1990s. Crimes against life and physical integrity—homicide, assault, rape— have risen sharply, and murders account for a growing percentage of unnatural deaths. In São Paulo, for example, the homicide rate jumped from 41.6 per 100,000 inhabitants in 1988 to 50.2 in 1993. Crimes against property—theft, robbery, fraud—are also on the rise. So is organized crime, especially drug trafficking and money laundering.

Worsening Violence

This endemic violence—embedded in a context of broad economic inequalities and a system of profoundly asymmetric social relations—is hardly a new phenomenon in the region. It has worsened over the past two decades, at least in part because neoliberal economic policies have widened the gap between rich and poor and doomed millions of Latin Americans to lives of poverty and social exclusion. But violence also stems from the continuation of a long tradition of authoritarian practices by elites against "non-elites"—practices that are often reproduced in social relations among poor people themselves. The return to democratic constitutionalism did little to eradicate the authoritarian practices embedded in the state and in society.

While the most egregious forms of human rights violations committed by the region's military regimes have been eliminated under civilian rule, the long-awaited democracies have not fulfilled their role as guardians of public order and protectors of the fundamental rights of all citizens. Consequently, the role of law remains precarious in many Latin American countries. In Brazil as elsewhere, the difference is that the victims are no longer political activists, many of them educated members of the middle class, whose opposition to the military regimes got them killed or brutally tortured. Today, the principal targets of arbitrary police behavior are the most defenseless and vulnerable groups in Brazilian society: rural workers, trade-union activists, minority groups and destitute children and adolescents, many of whom live in the streets. Arbitrary detention and torturing suspects are still common police practices. Extrajudicial killings are also shockingly common, including the assassination of street kids by off-duty police and the repression of rural workers struggling for land and labor rights in the Northeast. Much of this violence is fueled by ingrained discrimination against poor people and racial minorities, who constitute a high percentage of all homicide victims. The common denominator in all these cases is impunity. The failure to enforce the law not only makes a mockery of the principle of the equality of citizens before the law, but also makes it more difficult for governments to strengthen their legitimacy. It feeds the circle of officially sanctioned violence.

Latin American Inequality

Brazil, like other Latin American countries, is a society based on exclusion—a democracy without citizenship. The impact of globalization, coupled with the crises resulting from economic adjustment programs, separates the rich and poor as never before—"as if," says [professor] Hector Castillo Berthier, "they were oil and water." Countries with greater inequality—high rates of income concentration in upper-income groups—tend to have higher crime rates as well as higher levels of human rights violations. Brazil is a shocking example in this regard. A country with one of the most appallingly uneven distributions of income on the planet—in 1992, the richest 20% earned 32 times more than the poorest 20%—Brazil also has correspondingly high rates of crime and official violence. For example, worldwide, residents of Rio de Janeiro—along with Buenos Aires, Kampala and Pretoria—run the highest risk of having their homes broken into. And Brazil's militarized police forces, which come under the authority of state governments, are among the most deadly in the world. In 1992, for example, military police killed a record 1,470 civilians in São Paulo alone (compared to 27 police killings in New York City that year).

Those who are most affected by unemployment and most marginalized from the education system are also the most likely victims of both arbitrary police repression and common crime. In Brazil, for example, those most frequently victimized by violent crime live below the poverty line. The perpetrators of violent crimes, such as homicide, are usually from the same social strata as the victims. These crimes usually occur in poor neighborhoods and shantytowns. In fact, in most of Latin America's huge metropoli, there is a correlation between poor neighborhoods and death from violent causes, and a clear link exists between living conditions, violence and mortality rates.

This is the case in the shantytowns that dominate the landscape of almost all Latin American cities—*favelas* in Rio de Janeiro and São Paulo, *ranchos* in Caracas, *barriadas* in Lima, *campamentos* in Santiago, *ciudades perdidas* in Mexico City, *villas miserias* in Buenos Aires. In these "geographic and social pre-cities," says [French economist and sociologist] Ignacy Sachs, "the majority do not possess the minimum conditions of what could be called urban life." They lack adequate housing, have little access to work and income, and have difficulty obtaining basic services. Moreover, the state, particularly those institutions charged with maintaining peace and order, is rarely present in these "pre-cities," leaving the socially excluded to fend for themselves. In such a milieu, violence often becomes the mediator of daily social relations. Whenever the state's monopoly on legitimate violence is relaxed, survival may depend on an individual's ability to maintain his or her reputation by displaying a "credible threat of violence." "A seemingly minor affront is not merely a 'stimulus' to action, isolated in time and space," according to one study of violent behavior among poor classes in the United States. [According to professors of psychology Martin Daly and Margo Wilson,] "It must be understood within a larger social context of reputations, face, relative social status and enduring relationships." The offended party may feel the need to use violence to defend his or her status. In this sense, violence is, to a large extent, performance.

The Military Threat to Democracies

Despite the positive transitions that have taken place in Latin America, forms of militarized politics have emerged that have impeded the expansion of political freedoms, undermined the functioning of democratic institutions, and intimidated civil society. As long as structural and ideological legacies of the national security states remain, democratization is at risk. New internal security missions for military forces strengthen the most anti-democratic sectors within them and endanger the rights of citizens to protest, to influence their governments, or to fight for social and economic change. Legitimate opposition to the neoliberal model or to authoritarianism might again be identified as a threat to national security.

J. Patrice McSherry, *NACLA Report on the Americas*, November/December 1998.

This kind of inner-city violence may be the result of a "loss of structure in society." In other words, where social restraints have been loosened, violence is considered a legitimate means of resolving conflict and may actually be encouraged. But violence may also simply be a reaction by normal people to oppressive circumstances—be it poverty, the humiliation of unemployment, the pressure of organized crime or the arbitrary power of the police.

Young people are increasingly the victims of violent crime in large cities across Latin America. In São Paulo, an average of 102 youths between 15 and 24 years of age are murdered for every 100,000 inhabitants in that age range. In some poor neighborhoods, the figures for this age group reach epidemic proportions of up to 222 homicides per 100,000—more than ten times the national average. The degree to which young people are either victims or perpetrators of crime reveals the clear link between poverty and violence. This is not to say that there is a direct or mechanistic relationship between poverty and violent crime, but it is imperative to consider how inequality factors into the problem of growing crime in Latin America. As a result of economic-adjustment policies, many young people are unable to find jobs or pay university tuition fees. To compensate for their sense of marginality, many youths join street gangs, while others become involved in drug trafficking. Crime becomes a quick, easy means to climb the social ladder in a society in which legal and "respectable" channels for such mobility are largely cut off.

Latin American Governments Protect the Rich

Most analyses of crime, however, rarely make these distinctions. Even though most victims of crime are poor, the middle and upper classes perceive crime as a problem that only affects them. They see crime, moreover, as a constant threat from the lower classes—the "dangerous classes"—that must be held in check, whatever the cost. The police tend to act as border guards protecting the rich from the poor, and police violence remains cloaked in impunity because it is largely directed against these "dangerous classes" and rarely affects the lives of the well-to-do. Crime-prevention policies—especially those proposed during election time—are aimed less at controlling crime and delinquency than diminishing the fear and the insecurity of the ruling classes. Elite perceptions of the poor as part of the "dangerous classes" are fueled by a judicial system that prosecutes and convicts crimes committed by poor people, while the crimes of the elites go unchallenged. Middle-class crime—including corruption, financial scams, tax evasion and the exploitation of child or slave labor—are not perceived as threats to the status quo. The same is largely true for organized crime, including drug trafficking, money laundering and contraband, and even the very profitable arms trade, none of which are targets of consistent enforcement policies.

Even if the state no longer engages in systematic coercion against political dissidents, as it did during the dictatorships, it remains accountable for the repressive illegal practices of the police and the military which have survived the transitions to democracy. The state needs to work towards eradicating the impunity for official crimes to the same extent it tries to punish violent crimes committed by common criminals. In much of Latin America, the state has shown itself incapable—or, more likely, unwilling—to punish the criminal practices of state agents.

The problem, of course, is that the election of civilian governments does not necessarily mean that state institutions will operate democratically. [Professor and author] Guillermo O'Donnell referred to this as passing from the "first transition"—away from authoritarian rule toward elected civilian government—to the "second transition"—institutionalizing democratic practices at all levels of the state. In many post-dictatorship countries that lack a strong democratic tradition, the "second transition" has been immobilized by innumerable negative legacies of the authoritarian past.

This continuity suggests that, notwithstanding the political transitions to elected rule, the authoritarian regimes of the past and the new civilian democratic governments are barely differentiated expressions of the same system of domination by the same elites. Political democratization does not attack [as Pinheiro writes in a 1994 essay] "socially rooted authoritarianism." This authoritarianism also persists in what could be called the "microdespotisms" of daily life, manifested as racism, sexism and elitism. The combination of a lack of democratic controls over the ruling classes and the denial of rights to the poor reinforces historical social hierarchies. Civil rights and the rule of law are little more than smokescreens for domination. As a consequence, only the middle and upper classes actually benefit from the effective control that democracy exercises over the means of violence in the social interactions of daily life. For the poor and destitute majority of the population, unchecked power continues to be the most visible face of the state.

Periodical Bibliography

The following articles have been selected to supplement the diverse views presented in this chapter. Addresses are provided for periodicals not indexed in the *Readers' Guide to Periodical Literature*, the *Alternative Press Index*, the *Social Sciences Index*, or the *Index to Legal Periodicals and Books*.

George Ayittey	"Gun-Point Democracy in Africa," *Liberty*, September 1997. Available from the Liberty Foundation, 1018 Water St., Suite 201, Port Townsend, WA 98368.
John Chettle	"After the Miracle: Can South Africa Be a Normal State?" *National Interest*, Spring 1997.
Larry Diamond	"Restoring Democracy in Africa," *USA Today*, January 1998.
Howard W. French	"In Africa's Harsh Climate, Fruits of Democracy," *New York Times*, January 4, 1998.
Eduardo Galeano, interviewed by Helen Vatsikopoulos	"On Power and Privatization," *Toward Freedom*, November 1996. Available from 150 Cherry St. #3, Burlington, VT 05401.
John Hinshaw	"The Politics of South Africa: The Transition to Democracy," *Against the Current*, September/October 1998.
Samuel P. Huntington	"Democracy for the Long Haul," *Journal of Democracy*, April 1996.
Julius O. Ihonvbere	"Democratization in Africa," *Peace Review*, September 1997. Available from Carfax Publishing, 875-81 Massachusetts Ave., Cambridge, MA 02139.
Adrian Karatnycky	"The Decline of Illiberal Democracy," *Journal of Democracy*, January 1999.
Johanna McGeary	"An African for Africa," *Time*, September 1, 1997.
J. Patrice McSherry	"The Emergence of 'Guardian Democracy,'" *NACLA Report on the Americas*, November/December 1998.
Matt Moffett and Jonathan Friedland	"Larcenous Legacy," *Wall Street Journal*, July 1, 1996.
James Mwangi and Kaniaru Wacieni	"Demanding Democracy: The Future of the State in Africa," *Harvard International Review*, Spring 1997. Available from PO Box 401, Cambridge, MA 02238.
New York Times	"Undemocratic Elections," June 27, 1999.

CHAPTER 4

What Is the First World's Role in the Third World?

Chapter Preface

First World efforts to provide aid and military intervention to developing nations are not without their dangers. In 1993, American troops were sent to Somalia to rescue the nation from problems caused by drought and feuding warlords. The two-year mission was unsuccessful and deadly—forty-two American soldiers died, including eighteen U.S. Army Rangers who perished in a 1993 firefight with warlord Mohammed Farrah Aidid's troops. These and other fatalities have sparked debate over whether military intervention in Third World countries is a prudent action for developed countries to take.

Some analysts question the necessity of armed intervention, arguing that its goals are often misguided. Anna Simons, the associate director of African studies at UCLA, asserts that the problem with intervention is that it requires the intervening nation to choose sides. According to Simons, such partisanship is not necessarily humanitarian and does not reflect the fact that there are no innocent victims in ethnic conflicts. She explains: "Only outsiders view victims as innocent noncombatants worth protecting. Among locals, victims wouldn't be victims if they weren't viewed as enemies at worst and of no value at best." By taking sides, the troops sent during interventions also risk becoming victims, as the deadly battle with Somali warlords indicates.

Supporters of intervention acknowledge that while not every effort is successful, isolationism is an unwise policy. Andrew Purvis, a former correspondent in Africa for *Time* magazine, maintains that the West should not turn its back on Africa and states that intervening troops do not have to take sides. He offers examples of assistance that could be effective, such as establishing a permanent peacekeeping force and providing economic support to nations that have shown a willingness to establish democracies. Purvis contends: "A more vigorous and well-defined effort to prevent conflicts before they reach cataclysmic proportions would save some of the considerable cost of maintaining displaced multitudes in the future."

Military intervention is one role taken by First World nations in developing countries. In the following chapter, the authors consider what type of role, if any, the West should seek in the Third World.

1

"Foreign aid may well be the area of government about which average Americans have the most misconceptions."

U.S. Foreign Aid Benefits the Third World

J. Brian Atwood

In the following viewpoint, J. Brian Atwood maintains that the advantages of American foreign aid programs are not recognized by most citizens and government officials. He argues that foreign aid has helped finance medical and agricultural advances that have led to decreased child mortality and greater crop yields. In addition, Atwood contends that providing foreign aid benefits the American economy because developing nations are the fastest growing markets for U.S. exports. However, Atwood asserts, the government must provide an adequate budget to foreign aid programs—particularly the U.S. Agency for International Development (USAID)—in order to achieve these benefits. Atwood is the former administrator of USAID. He resigned in June 1999 and became the executive vice president of Citizens Energy Corporation.

As you read, consider the following questions:
1. According to the author, where does the United States rank in the amount of resources it allots to foreign assistance?
2. What do critics of foreign aid fail to recognize, in Atwood's opinion?
3. What does Atwood say is an enduring truth about foreign aid?

Excerpted from "World's Stability Requires U.S. Aid," by J. Brian Atwood, *Forum for Applied Research and Public Policy*, Winter 1997. Reprinted with the permission of the Forum for Applied Research and Public Policy.

Americans applaud when religious groups feed hungry children in Africa. They are grateful that humanitarian organizations immunize children around the world against debilitating diseases. They are gratified when American college professors pitch in to help former communist countries write laws that protect human rights and foster free markets. They are delighted when retired American executives travel to Latin American countries to advise struggling new businesses on how to set up accounting systems.

All of these activities demonstrate the values of a free and caring society and highlight America's can-do spirit and resourcefulness.

Foreign Aid Misconceptions

What many Americans do not realize, however, is that all of these caring, democratic, and entrepreneurial efforts receive a significant part of their funding through the U.S. Agency for International Development (USAID). The activities they applaud, in fact, are part of America's much derided foreign aid policy.

Poll after poll shows that the majority of Americans believe foreign aid expenditures are running up the federal deficit. They believe it is time for America to curtail its contribution and for other countries to do their share.

It turns out, however, that the same Americans who tell pollsters the United States spends too much on foreign aid also think foreign aid accounts for nearly 20 percent of the federal budget. When asked, they say that spending levels should be closer to 5 percent. They are shocked to learn that U.S. economic and humanitarian aid—which includes U.S. contributions to such multilateral organizations as the United Nations, World Bank, International Monetary Fund, and regional development banks—amounts to far less than 1 percent of the federal budget.

Indeed, cutting foreign aid out entirely—or doubling it— would barely make a discernable difference in the U.S. deficit.

Many Americans still think the United States is the most generous donor in the world. They might be embarrassed to learn that the United States ranks fourth in the world in the overall amount of resources it devotes to foreign assistance.

Japan, Germany, and France all outspend us annually, although our economy is six times larger than France's, more than four times larger than Germany's, and one-and-a-half times that of Japan's. In per-capita terms, U.S. foreign-assistance programs rank dead last among programs of all the industrialized nations, behind countries like Ireland and Portugal.

Foreign aid may well be the area of government about which average Americans have the most misconceptions. Such misconceptions threaten the future of a program that actually makes the world safer and more stable and creates a more competitive arena for American exports.

The Benefits of Foreign Aid

We can all take pride in the world's progress over the past half century. Death rates for children have been cut by half, and average life spans in developing countries have increased by more than 20 years, from 41 to 62. The ancient scourge of smallpox has been eliminated. Food production has outstripped the doubling of world population. Americans might be even prouder if they were aware of the critical role that their foreign aid dollars have played in these advances.

Taxpayers also might feel better if they realized that modern Americans benefit directly from our investments in foreign aid. Some 80 percent of the grants and contracts issued by USAID are directed through American firms, universities, and nonprofit groups. Moreover, many other benefits are derived from this investment. For instance, international agricultural research, supported in part by USAID, has produced high-yielding wheat and rice hybrids, which have prevented millions of people in developing countries from starving. This research has boosted yields in the United States as well.

A study by the International Food Policy Research Institute, based in Washington, D.C., found that the dividend paid to American farmers and consumers from those foreign aid investments has been up to $17 for each taxpayer dollar invested for rice and up to $190 for each taxpayer dollar for wheat. That return comes in the form of higher yields per acre for farmers using less pesticide per ton of food. For American consumers, it means lower prices than would otherwise have been possible.

Most of America's major trading partners once received U.S. aid. We get back far more—through American exports to these countries—than we invested in their development. In fact, the value of American exports in 1995 alone to Korea and Taiwan far exceeded the total of all the years of assistance these nations received from the United States. The fastest growing markets for U.S. exports are now in developing countries, which are the largest potential markets for the future.

Answering the Critics

Those who say foreign aid is a failure ignore this long honor roll of successes. They also fail to recognize that countries must reach a certain level of economic development before they can become markets for our goods and services. Critics often repeat the same complaints made when a Bush administration commission studying problems in the agency declared in 1992 that USAID was "hamstrung by waste, poor communication, and just plain mismanagement."

They ignore major reforms that followed, which transformed the chairman of the commission, George Ferris, from a once-harsh critic of USAID to a supporter of the reengineered agency. In fact, when Ferris returned three years after the commission's report to assess the progress that USAID had made, he declared, "This is the most remarkable transformation of a government agency I have ever seen."

As Ferris observed, USAID has come a long way. But the fact remains that we could have accomplished so much more with adequate funding and without having to constantly fight for our existence.

The Impact of Budget Reductions

Today American foreign aid is at its lowest level, in real terms, in 50 years. [Since 1994,] the budget of USAID has been cut by $1 billion in real terms for development and humanitarian relief, from $7.5 billion to $6.5 billion, and remained at roughly that level through fiscal year 1997. I am delighted that this downward trend seems about to end. The House and Senate have not reconciled their budget figures at this writing, but it appears that fiscal year 1998 will include modest increases for USAID. [USAID was given $6.977 billion.]

Having lost nearly 20 percent of its workforce, USAID has had to absorb the third-largest workforce reduction of all federal agencies. And USAID has closed 29 missions and curtailed long-term investments in key programs, including agriculture and economic development.

Budget reductions increasingly have determined the parameters within which our foreign policy can operate. Foreign aid is not the only area that has suffered. The State Department has been forced to close embassies and consulates even as the percentage of American goods and services that are exported has doubled in the face of growing global competition. Around the globe, America's diplomatic presence is simply drying up. Indeed, the amount of money the United States spends on diplomacy is at a record low. In 1985, international affairs made up 2.5 percent of the total budget. Since then the percentage has been cut in half—a far higher proportion than the much larger defense budgets have sustained.

The Budget for USAID (in $ millions)

Item	Fiscal Year 1998 (actual)
Development assistance	1,725
International disaster assistance	190
Credit programs	11
Operating expenses—USAID	479
Operating expenses—USAID/IG	29
Economic support fund	2,420
Eastern Europe	485
Former Soviet Union	771
Food for Peace	867
Total	6,977

U.S. Agency for International Development, *The Fiscal Year 1998 USAID Accountability Report.*

Former Secretary of Defense William Perry and General John Shalikashvili, chairman of the Joint Chiefs of Staff, know that defense and intelligence alone are not enough to provide a sound national security strategy. In an article they coauthored for *USA Today* in May 1995, titled "The Truth

About Foreign Aid," they expressed concern about proposed cuts in the budgets for diplomacy and foreign aid. The article insists that "when diplomacy fails, conflict often results. Whatever the cost of foreign aid, it's cheaper than military combat."

They recalled how aid to Europe through the Marshall Plan paid huge dividends in peace and security. "Today's foreign assistance budget is helping to finance another epic transition that will affect U.S. security for generations—the move from communism to democracy and free markets in Russia and Eastern Europe," they wrote. They concluded that "foreign aid, like defense spending, helps preserve our national security."

It would be tragic if, after emerging victorious from the long twilight of the Cold War, the United States were unable to meet the new challenges of the post–Cold War era because of public misconceptions about what foreign aid is and what it costs. History records the tragic result of America's withdrawal from world responsibilities after World War I. Indeed, we ultimately defeated communism largely because we resisted the call for disengagement after World War II. In today's world of global markets, instant communication, and missiles that can cross oceans in minutes, disengagement is simply not an option.

Aid Improves National Security

Ironically, the defense and intelligence communities seem to understand the role foreign aid plays in national security better than the public. For instance, the Defense Intelligence Agency has identified the ecological deterioration of Lake Victoria as a cause of potential instability in East Africa. Thirty million people who live near this huge lake are at risk of having their livelihoods and well-being compromised by an increasing mass of water hyacinths that threatens to cut off vital oxygen to fish and destroy a once-thriving fishing industry, depriving residents of an important source of protein.

Though environmental problems, even disasters, rarely result directly in the collapse of governments, ecological deterioration and crop failures—and the need for scapegoats in

166

times of economic distress—often exacerbate racial, tribal, and religious tensions that might otherwise have remained in check. Furthermore, famine and internal political and social conflicts often trigger mass migrations that can destabilize entire regions.

Defense Intelligence Agency analysts know that if the root causes of such problems go unaddressed—in this case the ecological deterioration of Lake Victoria—our military forces may be called upon to deal with the consequences a few years hence. The Defense Intelligence Agency understands that many problems cannot be resolved by U.S. military might, nor can the United States feel protected from these problems because they arise far from our shores.

Indeed, many of the adversaries the United States faces today will not yield to weapons. Neither nuclear arsenals nor oceans can shield us from viruses and pollution. The latest generation of fighter planes cannot defend us against global warming, nor can our aircraft carriers prevent the loss of biodiversity. Submarines cannot attack soil depletion or dwindling water resources that threaten food supplies. And even throngs of U.S. troops cannot prevent mass migrations of people fleeing natural and human-induced disasters and civil strife.

International diplomacy and economic development ultimately remain the cornerstones of our defense against nuclear proliferation and the poverty that breeds desperation. Such desperation makes people more vulnerable to demagogues who fan the flames of ethnic, religious, and tribal conflicts. The threats faced by the United States today are similar to the threats faced by all nations and all people. Without strong U.S. leadership and aid, these threats could undermine the very core of worldwide social and economic progress. We cannot ignore the forces that destabilize regions and create human and environmental catastrophes; we do so at our own peril.

Preventing Crises

[The 1990s] has seen the greatest flood of refugees in human history. As 1997 began, one in every 115 people on Earth was a refugee or displaced within his or her own country by war or natural disaster. The international community now spends about $4 billion a year on those 50 million refugees and displaced persons.

That total includes the costs of camps run by the United Nations High Commission on Refugees, the World Food Programme, and the International Red Cross as well as assistance from other private and governmental organizations. It does not include the cost for peacekeeping missions around the world. Those missions cost $5.4 billion in 1993 alone—which exceeds outlays for the previous 45 years combined.

One of the most enduring truths about foreign aid is that it is far cheaper to help people grow more food on their own farms than it is to try to feed people who have abandoned their homes in search of food or safety. It is much more expensive to provide make-shift shelter and prevent disease in refugee camps than it is to help people improve health and housing in their own villages.

The financial costs of political, social, and environmental crises are small compared to the costs in human suffering they cause. Indeed, these crises bear cruel dividends, including hatred, revenge, and loss of health, education, and income. Some of these consequences may continue to plague generations to come. In the final analysis, we pay an exceedingly high price for failing to intervene before a crisis comes. And crisis prevention is exactly what development programs are designed to achieve.

Foreign Aid and Democracies

Along with the unprecedented numbers of humanitarian crises, [the 1990s] has brought unprecedented opportunities to help strengthen fragile new democracies and bolster market economies. The majority of the world's nations—more than 60 percent, in fact—are now democracies, up from only 40 percent in 1983. The United States spent billions of dollars annually throughout the Cold War to spread democracy. Yet just when we have an unprecedented opportunity to help countries establish market democracies, assistance funding has been cut drastically.

The spirit of democracy that has swept the world is the true peace dividend from the end of the Cold War. But as with the fruits of any victory, this opportunity can be frittered away by failure to follow up on the gains we have achieved.

Most governments want to reform inefficient state-run economic systems and turn toward market-based systems, but few know how to effect such change. Reading the works of economist Adam Smith may build faith in the market place. It does not, however, put in place requisite financial and banking systems or provide the trained economists, the capital markets, or the skills needed to run the institutions of a market economy.

World population is growing by 1 billion people each decade, and most of this growth is taking place in developing countries. Benign neglect and increased trade will not meet the pressing needs of the poorest of these people. The poorest nations cannot successfully compete in the global economy, but they can succumb to the crises that produce internal bloodbaths and threaten to destabilize entire regions. And while the best intentions and most carefully designed and implemented programs will not prevent all crises, they can avert many of them.

> *"The belief that foreign capital can solve the problems of developing nations is a fatal conceit."*

U.S. Foreign Aid Does Not Benefit the Third World

L. Jacobo Rodriguez

American foreign aid has stymied the economic development of the Third World, L. Jacobo Rodriguez asserts in the following viewpoint. For example, he contends, farmers in developing countries are forced out of business by the influx of American food aid. Rodriguez also argues that, despite the claims of some foreign aid proponents, the postwar economic growth of Europe and Asia was not the result of U.S. financial assistance. He maintains that the United States can best encourage the development of poor nations by trading with foreign markets. Rodriguez is the assistant director of the Project on Global Economic Liberty at the Cato Institute in the District of Columbia. The project studies ways to transform former communist countries into market economies.

As you read, consider the following questions:
1. According to Peter Bauer, as quoted by the author, how is "Third World" defined?
2. In Rodriguez's opinion, why was West Germany able to improve its economy after World War II?
3. What American principles are exemplified by trade, according to the author?

Excerpted from "Myths and Realities," by L. Jacobo Rodriguez. This article appeared in the June 1997 issue of, and is reprinted with permission from, *The World & I*, a publication of The Washington Times Corporation, copyright ©1997.

In the twentieth century, the United States has helped the Western nations keep their freedom during two world wars and the Cold War. In the last 50 years, however, the U.S. government has unwittingly contributed to keeping citizens of Third World nations from enjoying freedom and the material prosperity that comes with it.

To understand that seeming irony, it is useful to remember that the Third World is neither an economic nor a geographical concept but a political one. As British economist Peter Bauer wrote, the Third World is "merely a name for the collection of countries whose governments . . . demand and receive official aid from the West."

By disbursing generous amounts of taxpayers' money to the governments of those countries the U.S. government has thwarted freedom and economic development in poor nations and allowed poverty to fester in much of the world.

The Goals of Foreign Aid

Since World War II, Washington has disbursed over $1 trillion (in 1996 constant dollars, or cd) in foreign aid, both bilaterally and through multilateral lending organizations such as the World Bank and the International Monetary Fund, in pursuit of a variety of foreign policy goals. Those goals have ranged from military assistance and political influence to humanitarian relief and economic development. In each case, the effectiveness of using U.S. economic aid must be evaluated separately.

According to congressional sources, U.S. military obligations to poor countries from 1946 to 1996 were more than $439 billion (cd). The effectiveness of military aid in preserving U.S. national security should be evaluated solely on the basis of whether that amount was the lowest possible expenditure for achieving that goal.

It is very unlikely, however, that even during the Cold War U.S. national security was at stake in every corner of the world, as the distribution pattern of U.S. military aid would lead one to believe. That strategy did, however, have a very destructive effect on the societies of the recipient countries because U.S. military aid strengthened the militaries of those countries.

It is quite obvious that the end of the Cold War and the demise of the Soviet Union have ended the military justification for sending millions of dollars to every corner of the world. Yet aid advocates continue to stress the need for military aid, which they consider a small price to pay for U.S. global leadership.

President Clinton, for instance, has defended the maintenance of a strong U.S. presence overseas by saying, "We did not win the Cold War to walk away and blow the peace on 'penny-wise, pound-foolish budgeting.' . . . For a pittance by American standards, we can make all the difference in the world. But we cannot do it for free."

Foreign Aid Does Not Benefit America

The political justification for foreign aid also arose during the Cold War. It was (and still is) in the national interest of the United States that underdeveloped nations prosper under a framework of democratic capitalism. It was wrongly assumed, however, that economic assistance would help the United States buy political influence.

As Bauer has explained, foreign aid led to the creation of anti-U.S. coalitions among developing nations, which demanded bribes (i.e., more foreign aid) not to go communist.

A 1995 study by Bryan Johnson, an analyst at the Heritage Foundation, shows that, even as recently as 1994, most recipients of U.S. foreign aid voted against the United States in the United Nations most of the time. That only shows how foreign aid has failed to buy political influence in developing countries. As with military aid, the end of the Cold War has made the political justification for foreign aid obsolete.

The Pitfalls of Humanitarian Relief

The technological advances of the twentieth century notwithstanding, natural calamities—from earthquakes to floods—still occur, sometimes with devastating consequences. Developing nations can be extremely vulnerable to those disasters because of their inferior infrastructure.

The generosity and goodwill of American citizens have always led them to assist those struck by such devastation, whether at home or on a faraway continent. Consequently, official humanitarian aid to provide short-term disaster relief, although not harmful, has often proved to be redundant.

While the effects of official short-term relief have been benign, unfortunately the same cannot be said of Food for Peace, or P.L. 480, the largest official program aimed at providing long-term relief. As Doug Bandow, a senior fellow at the Cato Institute, explains, "Food for Peace was created more to dump surplus American crops in foreign markets than to alleviate starvation; just 14 percent of the food shipments go to disaster-stricken areas."

The cost to the U.S. taxpayer of what essentially is a subsidy to American farmers has been approximately $3 billion per year since 1946. (Although Food for Peace was established in 1954, the U.S. government has been distributing food aid since World War II.)

The Recipe for Economic Freedom

With the end of the Cold War, the idea that economic freedom might play a prominent and supportive role in self-sustaining development has become a less "controversial" and "ideological" contention than it once seemed to be. Rule of law, including property and contract law; sound money; open markets; transparent and accountable government regulations—these are among the ingredients in the recipe for economic freedom. Since such qualities lower "transaction costs" and reduce the uncertainties facing ordinary economic agents, it should not be surprising that a relationship should link economic freedom and economic progress.

The fundamentals of economic freedom can be seen not only as a virtue in their own right, but as broadly conducive to sustained and self-sustaining material advance.

Nicholas Eberstadt, *Washington Times*, October 7, 1996.

The cost to the farmers of those countries where massive amounts of food have been dumped has been even higher, because the influx of cheap American foodstuffs into the local marketplaces has forced the majority of those farmers out of business. As a result, Food for Peace has tended to discourage agricultural development in poor countries.

Furthermore, where Food for Peace has actually provided famine relief, the famine has usually been the result of government recklessness in the first place. The clearest example is provided by Ethiopia's Mengistu regime, a longtime recipient of aid, which in the 1980s collectivized farms and forcefully relocated much of Ethiopia's population, resulting in widespread starvation in the mid 1980s. Thus, the fundamental problem with Food for Peace is that it offers relief for emergencies usually caused by bad government policies, thus providing a safety valve that allows the delay of market-oriented reforms.

Economic Development Myths

Advocates of foreign aid have long offered the promotion of economic growth as the main justification for international transfers. Unfortunately, more than five decades of Washington's assistance has done little to alleviate poverty in the less developed nations and much to increase the personal fortunes of Third World rulers.

Those developing nations that have attained high levels of economic growth, such as Chile, Taiwan, and South Korea, have done so despite foreign aid, not because of it. Indeed, their prosperity can be attributed to the implementation of market reforms that followed the end of large aid flows. Yet supporters of aid constantly point to those and a handful of other cases as conclusive evidence that aid works. A closer inspection reveals that aid success stories are based largely on myth.

Foreign aid myths. Inevitably, proponents of foreign aid invoke the Marshall Plan to justify continued or increased lending to any part of the developing world. The Marshall Plan made substantial funds available on concessional terms (about $12 billion from 1948 to 1952) to European countries to help with the postwar reconstruction. The notion that the program caused European development faces two problems.

First of all, it is inaccurate. In the case of West Germany, for instance, the reforms undertaken by Ludwig Erhard provide a more plausible explanation of that country's exceptional economic performance in the years following World War II. Beginning in 1948, Erhard greatly reduced tariffs, abolished price controls, slashed income tax rates from a top rate of 95 percent on incomes over $15,000 to a (still high) rate of 53 percent on incomes over $250,000, and fixed the deutsche mark to the dollar, which stopped inflation.

Second, and more important, even if the Marshall Plan had been the key to European recovery, it would still fail the relevancy test because institutional frameworks conducive to economic growth were already present in Europe after the war. That is definitely not the case in most developing nations today. As Bandow explains,

> The European people retained the legal, economic, educational, philosophical, and cultural infrastructure necessary for successful industrial economies. Most aid recipients, in contrast, need to generate these characteristics before creating the industrial infrastructure necessary for growth; development, not restoration, is the issue.

The Reasons for Asia's Success

But surely, supporters of aid claim, the exceptional growth rates of South Korea and Taiwan, which received substantial assistance from the United States in the 1950s and '60s, must be considered examples of aid success. While it is true that both countries received massive amounts of U.S. assistance during the 1950s and '60s, most of it was military aid, not economic.

Furthermore, a more credible explanation for the "Asian Miracle" is that the market-oriented reforms undertaken by the governments of the Asian Tigers are responsible for the dramatic increase in standards of living there. When U.S. development assistance to Taiwan ended in 1965, for example, the Taiwanese government was forced to seek a path toward self-sustaining economic growth.

And Hong Kong, the most successful of the Tigers, received no assistance from the United States between 1946 and 1996, with the exception of $220 million in food aid. (Official assistance to Hong Kong from other sources was also negligible during that period.) Per capita income there went from $2,247 in 1960 to $17,832 in 1994 (in 1985 U.S. dollars).

Even Israel, the largest recipient of U.S. aid since World War II ($107 billion cd), can hardly be considered a 100 percent success story. In 1996 the Institute for Advanced Strategic and Political Studies, an Israeli think tank, complained,

Almost one-seventh of the GDP comes to Israel as charity. This has proven economically disastrous. It prevents reform, causes inflation, fosters waste, ruins our competitiveness and efficiency, and increases the future tax burden on our children who will have to repay the part of the aid that comes as loans.

With its well-educated population, Israel could have a thriving free-market economy and be capable of providing for its own defense. Instead, according to Hoover Institution scholar Alvin Rabushka, "Israel ranks at the bottom of all Western countries on every measure of economic freedom." It has become an aid junkie.

A Flawed Foreign Aid Policy

Foreign aid realities. The economic argument for foreign aid is rooted in the belief that underdeveloped nations need sufficiently large infusions of foreign capital to escape the poverty trap set by low levels of income, domestic savings, and foreign reserves. (If that notion were true, however, no society would ever have been able to develop and prosper, a point that Bauer has made incessantly.) Given those problems and the supposed absence of well-functioning private capital markets, it was widely assumed after World War II, when foreign aid programs were first established, that only the public sector would be able to provide the needed capital.

The policy prescription derived from that false belief was and remains flawed. To determine whether the policy has been successful, one ought to look at the "graduation rate"—that is, the number of developing nations that U.S. foreign aid has pulled out of poverty.

The record is dismal, especially in sub-Saharan Africa and the Indian subcontinent. Countries in those regions have been receiving huge amounts of foreign aid for more than three decades. There is little indication that they are more prosperous today than they were when they began receiving aid from the U.S. Agency for International Development (U.S. AID) and other taxpayer-supported lending institutions.

Worse, much of that aid, both bilateral and multilateral, has served to prop up the regimes of brutal dictators throughout the Third World, from Tanzania's Julius Nyerere to Haiti's "Baby Doc" Duvalier to Zaire's Mobutu Sese

Seko, who, as of press time, is barely clinging to power as his country collapses. [In May 1997, Seko fled the capital Kinshasa, Laurent Kabila declared himself head of state.]

But even in the case of more benign regimes, foreign aid has allowed governments to continue their statist policies, conceal the harmful effects of those policies, and delay the implementation of reforms that would lead to sustainable economic growth. For instance, Nicaragua has received more than $3 billion in aid since the Sandinistas were ousted in 1990; yet per capita income in that resource-rich nation is, after Haiti, the second lowest in the Western Hemisphere—even lower than Cuba's. The Chamorro administration that replaced the Sandinistas as well as the new government of Arnoldo Alemán have not implemented a credible reform program, which, not surprisingly, has led foreign (and domestic) investors to look elsewhere. In practice, foreign aid is a reward for bad economic policies and government mismanagement.

Domestic Policies Are Important

The belief that foreign capital can solve the problems of developing nations is a fatal conceit, because it ignores the crucial role of domestic institutions and policies. As Professor Mancur Olson Jr. of the University of Maryland explains, "The only remaining plausible explanation is that the great differences in the wealth of nations are mainly due to the differences in the quality of their institutions and economic policies."

To the extent that the governments of developing nations have opened their economies, established the rule of law, and protected property rights, they have provided the necessary institutional framework under which domestic capital can be accumulated. The fate of those nations does not depend on large transfers of foreign aid.

In addition, the dramatic increase in private capital flows to developing nations (from $44 billion in 1990 to more than $240 billion in 1996) can be attributed to the institutional reforms that many developing nations have undertaken in the past decade. Those reforms provide greater assurance to private foreign investors that the success of their investments will depend on market forces, not government power and coercion.

Not to be deterred by more than 50 years of failure, U.S. AID and the other foreign aid bureaucracies of the industrialized world continue to support the economic basket cases of the world with about $60 billion in loans and grants annually. Unfortunately, while admitting to their own shortcomings in the past (J. Brian Atwood, administrator of U.S. AID, has even conceded that his agency was "on the road to mediocrity or worse"), supporters of aid continue to offer new justifications for maintaining their programs in the future.

Chief among those are the notions that foreign aid is necessary to promote market reforms in the former communist countries of eastern Europe and is a vital component of "nation building." To that end, the Clinton administration has requested $19.5 billion for international affairs for fiscal year 1998, including $1.6 billion for "democracy-building" programs. [Approximately $19 billion was budgeted.]

Trade Is the Solution

In 1958 Nobel economist Milton Friedman wrote, "Though foreign economic aid may win us some temporary allies, in the long run it will almost surely retard economic development and promote the triumph of Communism. It is playing into our enemies' hands, and should be abolished."

Fifty years of failed development planning confirm the wisdom of those words. It is time for Washington to posit a new relation with developing countries based on open markets and leave government-to-government foreign aid where it belongs—in the dustbin of failed development policy.

Trade, not aid, promotes prosperity and freedom. Trade, not aid, is consistent with American principles of self-reliance and individual responsibility. Let's help people in poor countries help themselves, not reward governments for keeping their people in poverty.

| "*Angola . . . is but one of many African nations where concrete, definitive and consistent U.S. engagement is badly needed.*"

The United States Should Take a More Active Role in Africa

Ileana Ros-Lehtinen

The United States lacks a coherent strategy in Africa, Ileana Ros-Lehtinen argues in the following viewpoint. She contends that the United States needs to implement a proactive policy that encourages democracy, trade, development, and respect for human rights. Ros-Lehtinen maintains that American leadership is especially important in Angola, Zaire, and Rwanda. Ros-Lehtinen, a Florida Republican, is the chair of the House International Relations Committee's subcommittee on International Economic Policy and Trade.

As you read, consider the following questions:
1. What were the results of the border camps the United States established in Zaire, according to Ros-Lehtinen?
2. What are some of Angola's resources, as listed by the author?
3. In the author's opinion, how does the world respond when the United States leads?

Excerpted from "Needed: Proactive African Engagement," by Ileana Ros-Lehtinen, *The Washington Times*, December 13, 1996. Reprinted with the permission of *The Washington Times*.

179

With Somalia* still haunting the Clinton administration, U.S. officials continued to delay responding to the plight of the Rwandan refugees in Zaire. It was not until public concern and international pressure became so overwhelming that the U.S. reluctantly decided to join an intervention force to help open humanitarian corridors between Rwanda and Zaire.

Now, the administration must be breathing a sigh of relief, as it appears that the military force envisioned will no longer be necessary—thanks to the initiative of the refugees themselves, who broke free from the Hutu militias and are returning to Rwanda. The mission is now a humanitarian one focusing on helping the Rwandan government manage the reintegration of refugees into society.

An Incoherent Policy

Observers of the continent agree that this . . . Central Africa crisis was both avoidable and predictable. In 1994, when the Hutu refugees came streaming into Zaire in fear of retribution from the Tutsi government, the international community, including the United States, did not have the courage and determination to tackle the underlying problems that forced the refugees' departure. Its solution was to set up way stations for the refugees. These border camps sparked inevitable tensions between Zaire and Rwanda, allowed the Hutu militias the protection of a human shield, and cost the international community hundreds of millions of dollars.

I raise this example not to place blame for the Zaire/ Rwanda crisis, but to highlight a problem endemic to the U.S. approach to Africa—the lack of a coherent preemptive strategy to avoid further conflicts combined with a reluctance by the U.S. to become substantively involved in the continent. This is not just a problem for the Clinton administration, but one that needs to be addressed by all branches of the government.

U.S. policy makers have been virtually paralyzed by the

*The U.S. Marines participated in a 2-year intervention in Somalia that ended in 1995. The intervention sought to rescue the nation from drought and feuding warlords but did not succeed. Forty-two American soldiers and more than 100 peacekeepers died.

ghosts of Somalia past—focusing on the path of least resistance, losing sight of the goals and what the U.S. was trying to accomplish in the first place. As a result, the policy is disheveled and the U.S. appears indecisive, indifferent to the suffering of others, and most troublesome, unwilling to lead.

America Must Become More Engaged in Africa

As my colleagues in the Congress know, I am not one to argue for the deployment of U.S. forces in Africa, or anywhere, every time tensions erupt. It would be irresponsible to send American troops into conflict based on knee-jerk assessments. On the contrary, what I am calling for—and it is a theme I have repeated many times and will continue to emphasize—is for more effective, proactive engagement in Africa, in the hopes of preventing the need for American troop involvement in the future. I am suggesting a policy that looks at promoting the fundamentals: democracy, respect for human rights, trade and development.

Zaire and Rwanda both need to be approached from this perspective. We cannot afford to ignore these two countries once the immediate crisis goes away. We must be active participants in the discussion to establish a new order, both within and between the two countries. Unlike France and other European powers, the U.S. has no historical agenda and is perceived as an honest broker. Such an initiative will take political and financial capital, but nothing compared to that which will need to be expended if the U.S. sits idly by and maintains the unstable status quo.

Zaire and Rwanda, however, are not the only African countries that require a pro-active U.S. policy. Zaire's southern neighbor, Angola, also needs the active engagement of the United States. With its wealth of oil, diamonds, fertile land and other natural resources, Angola has the potential to be one of the richest countries of the continent. It is the last piece in the Southern African puzzle, given Namibia's independence and South Africa's transition.

Triumphs and Troubles in Angola

Today, Angola is moving toward peace because the United States government initially made a decision to engage and to remain engaged. Under the leadership of the special envoy to Angola, Ambassador Paul Hare, the United States had maintained a relatively even-handed policy in negotiating a peace between the government of Angola and Uniao Nacional para a Independencia Total de Angola (UNITA). However, now, when Angola has reached its most critical juncture, the United States is showing the same signs of fatigue and confusion that it showed in Rwanda in 1994.

For two years, U.S. negotiators worked with the United Nations and the government of Russia and Portugal to implement the Lusake Protocol, the blueprint for Angola's peace process. The agreement calls for the demobilization of UNITA forces, the return of government troops to their barracks, the formation of a national army, and the establishment of a government of national unity. While there have been delays in the process, notable progress has been made, including a nation-wide cease fire that has held.

Aid to Africa Can Benefit America

Although development assistance rarely changes history dramatically, it can do significant good in a significant number of places. And it can do good in ways that help us to reinvent ourselves as a nation in the context of a more interconnected world, while also promoting vital security interests. A growing African middle class, for instance, would constitute an enormous market for American products. An Africa in which viruses could be monitored and controlled would preserve AIDS as a singularity rather than a harbinger of more pandemics. Given that disease is affected by poverty, migration, and environmental trends, helping Africa is strategically important if only in terms of cold self-interest.

Robert D. Kaplan, *Atlantic Monthly*, August 1996.

Nevertheless, in September [1996], the Clinton administration began taking some steps that could place the long-term stability of Angola in jeopardy. These suggest a knee-jerk reaction by the administration to the February [1997] deadline for the withdrawal of U.N. peacekeepers, rather than a carefully thought out policy to ensure a successful resolution to the peace process in Angola.

First, the administration began to back away from its

even-handed policy, deciding that the best way to accelerate the process was to squeeze UNITA and isolate it politically. Second, and of more concern, the United States placed little emphasis on what is to happen in Angola after the Lusaka Protocol.

The U.S. cannot afford to take its eye off the ball. The peace process is only a bridge. The Lusaka Protocol will be meaningless unless it leads Angola to a democratic society and toward economic growth. The U.S. did not invest its human and financial resources to fail in its commitment to bring multi-party democracy to Angola. Our goal must be to bring Angola into the group of newly emerging democracies in Southern Africa. We should not disengage until the mission is completed.

The U.S. Must Lead

Again, Angola, like Zaire and Rwanda, is but one of many African nations where concrete, definitive and consistent U.S. engagement is badly needed. There are many others, such as Sudan, Mauritania, and Nigeria, whose future development into free and democratic nations—into countries that safeguard civil liberties and respect human rights—also depends on the level of U.S. interest, commitment and action.

Some would argue that the United States has no business in Africa and that its leadership would be perceived as interference. However, history has proven that when the United States leads, the world does not rebel, it applauds. The message is clear: the U.S. should lead, needs to lead, must lead.

"In countries like Uganda, the development taking place is in the interest of the imperialists."

U.S. Involvement in Africa Is Imperialist

Revolutionary Worker

In the following viewpoint, the *Revolutionary Worker* contends that the United States' involvement in Africa since the 1960s has led to the exploitation and oppression of much of Africa. The newspaper argues that foreign aid and investment benefits the local capitalists in Uganda and other countries and fails to help the masses. In addition, the newspaper asserts that American support of African dictatorships has further damaged the continent. The *Revolutionary Worker* is a weekly newspaper published by the U.S. Revolutionary Communist Party.

As you read, consider the following questions:

1. What are the *Revolutionary Worker*'s criticisms of the African Growth and Opportunity Act?
2. How has foreign investment affected Nigeria, according to the newspaper?
3. What role has the United States played in Zaire, as stated by the *Revolutionary Worker*?

Excerpted from "Africa: Clinton's Colonial Roadshow," *Revolutionary Worker*, April 5, 1998. Reprinted with the permission of RCP Publications. Greenhaven Press, Inc. has retitled this article and added all subheads and the cartoon.

At the end of March [1998], the U.S. presidential road show traveled through one of the most poverty-stricken areas of the world as Bill Clinton toured five African countries south of the Sahara Desert. Eighteen of the world's 20 poorest countries are located here. Excluding South Africa, the total gross national product (GNP) of all countries in sub-Saharan Africa—where 600 million people live—is about the same as the GNP of Belgium, a well-off European country with a population of only 10 million. Every day, 10,000 children die in this region from preventable diseases.

Clinton's trip was advertised as a move toward a "new relationship" between the U.S. and Africa, based on "mutual interest and mutual respect." Clinton said that the U.S. wants to promote investment and trade in order to help these countries become self-reliant, climb out of poverty and undergo a "renaissance." And he performed his trademark "I feel your pain" routine—expressing regret for the U.S. role in the slave trade, apartheid, and the 1994 massacres in Rwanda.

American Imperialism

But behind all the talk of a "new relationship" is the reality of imperialist greed and manipulation. While Clinton claims that the African countries are "equal partners," the U.S. is attempting to strengthen the profoundly *unequal* relationship between U.S. imperialist power and the oppressed countries of Africa.

Take a look at the African Growth and Opportunity Act now being considered by the U.S. Congress. This legislation was highlighted during the trip as a key part of the U.S. plans for Africa. The bill calls on African countries to sell state-owned companies to private investors and take other measures to "liberalize" the economy and get more in line with "free market" capitalism. Governments that follow this economic formula would be rewarded with lower tariffs and higher quotas for exports to the U.S. [The measure did not pass in 1998 in the Senate. In 1999 it was approved by the House. As of this writing, action had not been taken in the Senate.]

This is crude extortion, imperialist style. The U.S. is threatening the sub-Saharan countries: Make it easier for foreign capitalists to come in and buy up the privatized com-

panies, extract mineral resources and exploit labor cheaply—
or you'll find it hard to sell your exports in the U.S.

Randall Robinson of TransAfrica put it very sharply:
"This bill nakedly and unqualifiedly promotes the interests
of American business. It should be called The African Re-
colonization Act, because the U.S. and Europe have the
money and would grab up the assets."

Capitalism Has Not Helped Uganda

One of the countries Clinton visited was Uganda. The U.S.
praises Ugandan leader Yoweri Museveni for his "free market
reforms." Museveni has sold off government-owned industries
to private capitalists, laid off workers, raised taxes and taken
other measures that have earned the approval of the U.S. government, the International Monetary Fund (IMF) and the
World Bank. The U.S. points to Uganda's high rate of economic growth as proof that Museveni's policies are a success.

But this capitalist growth and development benefits only
a small section of the elite in Uganda—while the country
overall remains one of the poorest on earth, with per capita
income of $260 a year. In a country ravaged by AIDS, the
government's annual spending for health amounts to only $3
per person. In preparation for Clinton's visit, the police in
the Ugandan capital of Kampala kicked out hundreds of
beggars, street kids and the disabled from downtown streets.

Museveni says that he wants foreign investment in
Uganda, not foreign aid, in order to make the country more
self-reliant. But a major part of Museveni's economic "success" story is actually based on aid from the U.S. and other
major powers—who have a stake in upholding Uganda as a
"free market model" for other Third World countries. The
World Bank and the IMF provide loans, and foreign aid pays
for about 46 percent of the national budget of Uganda.

How can a country be moving toward self-reliance—
when almost half the government budget comes from imperialist pockets? Uganda is indeed a "model"—of imperialist
penetration and control.

Replacing foreign aid with more foreign investment is
definitely not a road to self-reliance. Nigeria is a case in
point. Huge amounts of foreign investments have poured

into this country. But these investments are directed toward the relentless pursuit of oil profit. All other aspects of the economy have been subordinated and sacrificed to the oil industry. Nigeria has built up an external debt of $35 billion, putting this country's economy at the mercy of foreign lenders. Nigeria serves as a major transportation point for heroin traffic from Southeast Asia to Europe and the U.S.—and this drug trade is a big part of this economy. And pollution has devastated the lives of the Ogoni people who live in the oil production areas.

Kirk Anderson. Reprinted with permission.

The problem in sub-Saharan Africa—or in any other oppressed country—is not that more foreign investment is needed, or that foreign investment is not used well. The problem is the investments themselves.

These investments—and the capitalist development they promote—are based on super-exploitation. Investment capital comes covered with blood—the blood of the peasants in Mexico forced off the land through the North American Free Trade Agreement (NAFTA) treaty, of the women working for pennies a day in Indonesian sweatshops, of the gold miners digging under deadly conditions in South Africa. Foreign investors do not come into countries like Uganda with the intention of helping the people—they come in search of low-cost labor to exploit and valuable resources to plunder.

Imperialist investment, trade and aid do promote a certain kind of development in oppressed countries. But imperialism twists and distorts the economy and society of these countries and prevents them from developing in an all-around way that benefits the masses of people. Capitalist development causes severe polarization—between the small top layer of the rich and the vast majority of poor, between the concentrated wealth of the city and the extreme poverty of the countryside.

As Maoist political economist Raymond Lotta points out, "Economic growth is not, in and of itself, good. The question is what kind of development? And who is this development for?" In countries like Uganda, the development taking place is in the interest of the imperialists and the local ruling class of big capitalists.

American Crimes Against Africa

Clinton claimed during the trip that "perhaps the worst sin America ever committed about Africa was the sin of neglect." He said that the U.S. intends to correct this by engaging more closely in Africa. This is a cynical attempt to whitewash the many crimes committed by the U.S. in Africa.

One sharp example of what U.S. "engagement" has *already* meant for Africa is the Congo (Zaire). Under the Democratic Kennedy administration, the CIA was deeply involved in the 1961 assassination of radical nationalist leader Patrice Lumumba. The murder of Lumumba was a key part of U.S. moves to elbow out the old-line European colonial powers in Africa and replace them with U.S. neocolonialism. Later, the U.S. backed the rise of the Mobutu dictatorship to power. During the '70s and '80s the U.S. sent billions of dollars in aid to build up Mobutu's military and prop up his regime. Meanwhile, Mobutu looted the economy and maintained his rule through brutal repression. [In 1997,] as the Mobutu regime crumbled, the Clinton administration backed the rise of Laurent Kabila as the new strongman for U.S. interests.

In South Africa, the U.S. supported the racist apartheid

regime for many years under the policy of "constructive engagement." In Angola and Mozambique, the U.S. backed counterrevolutionary armies waging reactionary wars. The U.S. sent troops to Somalia in 1994 under the guise of a "humanitarian mission"—but it quickly became clear that these soldiers were a bullying army of occupation. These are only a very few of the numerous ugly deeds the U.S. has carried out in Africa.

During the '70s and '80s, the U.S. moves in sub-Saharan Africa were very much connected to the worldwide contention with the rival imperialist bloc headed by the Soviet Union. After the fall of the Soviet Union, this region became less important strategically for U.S. policy makers. But now, the U.S. is making a new push to tighten its hold over this area of the world—at the expense of other powers like France.

Aside from more deeply exploiting the economies of these countries, the U.S. is also forging new military alliances to protect its interests. The Clinton administration's African Crisis Response Initiative provides standardized military training and equipment to a number of countries in the region. Senegal and Uganda, two of the countries Clinton visited, have already signed on—and Washington is trying to get South Africa to join.

Clinton went to Africa posing as a "contrite" leader of a world power now eager to help the African people. But while Clinton expressed regret for the slave trade, the system he represents has criminalized a whole generation of youth in the U.S. Clinton claimed to sympathize with the survivors of the massacres in Rwanda—but the U.S. government waged a cold-blooded genocidal war on Iraq and continues to kill thousands of Iraqi children each month with economic sanctions. Clinton joined Nelson Mandela to visit Robbens Island, where Mandela was held prisoner for two decades under apartheid—as the Jericho '98 march in Washington, D.C. denounced the persecution of political prisoners in the U.S. itself.

Clinton's pledge to get the U.S. more "engaged" in sub-Saharan Africa can bring nothing positive for the masses in these countries. More U.S. involvement only means more imperialist intervention, domination and intrigue—and more oppression for the people.

"Institutions that have helped Africans survive for centuries cannot be that deficient."

Africa Does Not Need Western Assistance

George B.N. Ayittey

In the following viewpoint, George B.N. Ayittey asserts that Africa should develop solutions based on traditional institutions, such as the counsel of tribal elders, rather than rely on foreign assistance. He argues that the traditional form of government in African villages allowed people to have an open and fair debate and reach a decision by consensus. Ayittey is the president of the Free Africa Foundation, which promotes development and democracy in Africa, and the author of *Africa in Chaos*, the book from which this viewpoint is taken.

As you read, consider the following questions:
1. What is the definition of the Swahili word *majimbo*?
2. According to Ayittey, what are the five steps that must be taken to solve a problem?
3. How did South Africa achieve its transition to a multiracial democracy, as stated by the author?

Excerpted from *Africa in Chaos*, by George B.N. Ayittey. Copyright ©1998 by George B.N. Ayittey. Reprinted with the permission of St. Martin's Press, LLC.

T he most maddening and unfathomable aspect of African reform is the fact that the very solutions required to save the continent are in Africa itself—in its own backyard. . . .

All Africa needs to do is to return to its roots and build on and modernize its own indigenous institutions. There is now a greater awareness of the need to reexamine Africa's own heritage. A return to traditional institutions will ensure not only peace but stability as well:

> Malians are quick to remind visitors that they were a nation long before they embraced democracy. Their 12 ethnic groups governed themselves for centuries before French colonization. Each ethnic group governed a region of the [Mali] empire. The governors of each region had to work together to preserve economic and political balance. The result: one of Africa's more stable and powerful empires.
>
> Such history has helped Mali resist ethnic tensions: When the Tuaregs of northern Mali rebelled against this government, they found no allies among the other ethnic groups.
>
> "Ethnicity cannot be manipulated in this society," said educator Lalla Ben Barkar. "The people may be from the north or the south, but in the end they realize they are one nation, and that is Mali." (*The Washington Post*, 24 March 1996, A28)

The Benefits of Traditional Institutions

According to Carl M. Peterson and Daniel T. Barkely, a reason why Somalia imploded is that "The previous government [Siad Barre's] failed to incorporate the institutional aspects of Somalia's indigenous culture into a functioning national body. . . . [Therefore] a stable, viable and fair political system must comprise the essential characteristics of Somalia's complex society. This means revitalizing indigenous institutions, restoring traditional powers and giving clans a legitimate outlet for political expression."

The traditional institutions, often rejected as "outmoded," can be useful. Indeed, this was exactly what was found by the multinational force that was sent into Somalia in 1993 to maintain peace and ensure delivery of relief food supplies to famine victims. The centralized government structure and other institutions established by the elites, such as schools, the postal service, and the central bank had all collapsed. But Somalia's traditional form of local government survived, and the U.S.-led military force tried to use it to revive the others. In the traditional system, decision is taken by clan elders, gray-haired men who have won inherited status in their communities as scholars, clerics and business leaders. "'They represent legitimacy in this country,' said Colonel Serge Labbe, the commander of Canadian forces, who meets frequently with elders to discuss how to end lawlessness, reopen schools and generally restore some degree of normal life. 'They're considered to be wise, almost supernatural in what they say.'"

Institutions that have helped Africans survive for centuries cannot be that deficient. At least, they are superior to the hastily imported systems that could not last for even 30 years. According to [author Christopher] Hitchens (1994), "The Swahili word for this concept, now coming back into vogue after a long series of experiments with foreign models, is *majimbo*. It stands for the idea of local initiative and trust in traditional wisdom." Adebayo Adedeji, former executive secretary of U.N. Economic Commission for Africa and director of the African Center for Development and Strategic Studies in Nigeria, would agree: "Unfortunately, the leadership that took over from the departing colonial authorities did not go back to our past to revive and revitalize our democratic roots. They took the line of least resistance and convenience and continued with despotism, autocracy, and authoritarianism. But the basic democratic culture is still there."

The Asian Model

E.F. Kolajo of Thoyandou, South Africa, concurred: "The Japanese, Chinese, and Indians still maintain their roots, and they are thriving as nations. Africa embraces foreign cultures at the expense of its own, and this is why nothing seems to work for us." In fact, according to *The Bangkok Post*, "Japan's postwar success has demonstrated that modernization does not mean Westernization. Japan has modernized spectacularly, yet remains utterly different from the West. Economic success in Japan has nothing to do with individualism. It is the fruit of sheer discipline—the ability to work in groups and to conform."

In view of their success, African leaders have been heading off in droves on tours of Asian countries, "Hoping to copy blueprints that allowed some Asian countries to leap from poverty to relative prosperity in little more than a generation, more and more African leaders are heading off these days on tours of countries like Singapore, Malaysia, Thailand and Korea. And along with their economic recipes, these leaders are returning home with authoritarian political notions."

It is hoped that the twenty-first century will find them heading off to Jupiter on a one-way ticket!

Reaching a Consensus

[There are] five steps that must be followed to solve a problem: (1) expose the problem; (2) diagnose its causes; (3) prescribe a solution; (4) implement a solution; and (5) monitor the solution. . . . When a crisis erupted in an African village, the chief and the elders would summon a village meeting. There the issue was debated by the people until a consensus was reached. During the debate, the chief usually made no effort to manipulate the outcome or sway public opinion. Nor were there bazooka-wielding rogues intimidating or instructing people on what they should say. People expressed their ideas openly and *freely* without fear of arrest. Those who cared participated in the decision-making process. No one was locked out. Once a decision had been reached by consensus, it was binding on all, including the chief.

In recent years, this indigenous African tradition has been revived by pro-democracy forces in the form of "national conferences" to chart a new political future in Benin, Cape Verde Islands, Congo, Malawi, Mali, South Africa, and Zambia. Benin's nine-day "national conference" began on 19 February 1990, with 488 delegates, representing various political, religious, trade union, and other groups encompassing the broad spectrum of Beninois society. The conference, whose chairman was Father Isidore de Souza, held "sovereign power" and its decisions were binding on all, including the government. It stripped President Matthieu Kerekou of power, scheduled multiparty elections and ended 17 years of autocratic Marxist rule.

Congo's national conference had more delegates (1,500) and lasted longer than three months. But when it was over in June 1991, the 12-year-old government of General Denis

Sassou-Nguesso had been dismantled. The constitution was rewritten and the nation's first free elections were scheduled for June 1992. Before the conference, Congo was among Africa's most avowedly Marxist-Leninist states. A Western business executive said, "The remarkable thing is that the revolution occurred without a single shot being fired . . . [and] if it can happen here, it can happen anywhere."

Community Efforts Throughout Africa

In Mogadishu and throughout Somalia, . . . voluntary community efforts, often uniting women's groups and traditional elders, are providing security and services, and pressing for genuine peace negotiations. Somalis say they are freer in many ways than their vaunted neighbors in Ethiopia and Eritrea. They are relearning how to govern and take care of themselves. A similar phenomenon has been well documented in the former Zaire, which had also become a virtual anarchy, as Mobutu's grip on power became weaker. Community groups throughout the country sprang up to repair roads, maintain prisons, hire traffic police, and promote human rights. Now that Congolese have tasted freedom and self-reliance, Laurent Kabila will find it much more difficult to impose a new dictatorship, if that is what he intends. Throughout the continent, Africans have long exercised the so-called "exit option." They have found African solutions for the problem of an unresponsive, nonexistent or repressive state, filling the gaps as best they can with whatever resources are available. It would be a shame if America continued to prop up the dictators, rather than find ways to encourage the creative efforts of grassroots communities.

Dave Peterson, *Washington Quarterly*, Summer 1998.

In South Africa, the vehicle used to make that difficult but peaceful transition to a multiracial democratic society was the Convention for a Democratic South Africa. It began deliberations in July 1991, with 228 delegates drawn from about 25 political parties and various anti-apartheid groups. The de Klerk government made no effort to "control" the composition of CODESA. Political parties were not excluded; not even ultra-wing political groups, although they chose to boycott its deliberations. CODESA strove to reach a "working consensus" on an interim constitution and set a date for the

March 1994 elections. It established the composition of an interim or transitional government that would rule until the elections were held. More important, CODESA was "sovereign." Its decisions were binding on the de Klerk government. De Klerk could not abrogate any decision made by CODESA—just as the African chief could not disregard any decision arrived at the village meeting.

Clearly, the vehicle exists—in Africa itself—for peaceful transition to democratic rule or resolution of political crisis. But the leaders in most African countries either are not interested or seek to control the outcome of such national/constitutional conferences.

"Most of the UN's financial and human resources are dedicated to development."

The United Nations Plays a Central Role in Third World Development

James Gustave Speth

In the following viewpoint, James Gustave Speth contends the United Nations has helped improve the quality of life in developing nations. He asserts that the UN is an essential contributor to Third World development for many reasons, including its national and commercial neutrality and its universal presence. Speth argues that the UN development programs should be strengthened to prevent the poverty and unemployment that often lead to violent conflicts. Speth is the Dean of the School of Forestry and Environmental Studies at Yale University and the former head of the United Nations Development Programme. This viewpoint was originally an address Speth gave in February 1996 before the World Affairs Forum.

As you read, consider the following questions:
1. How much money does the UN provide each year for development assistance, according to Speth?
2. In the author's view, what are the benefits of the UN's neutrality?
3. According to Speth, what will occur if the UN is made into a stronger human development agency?

Excerpted from "The U.S. and the U.N.: Back to the Future," by James Gustave Speth, *Christian Social Action*, September 1996. Reprinted with the permission of *Christian Social Action*.

The United Nations has a special role in development assistance. Though one would hardly know it from media coverage of the United Nations, which focuses on peacekeeping efforts, most of the UN's financial and human resources are dedicated to development. Through programs in 173 countries and territories, the UN system provides about $5 billion in assistance each year. Surprisingly, the UN's funds and specialized agencies provide slightly more official development assistance than the Bretton Woods institutions (the World Bank and the International Monetary Fund). Moreover, because the United Nations makes grants, not credits, there is a substantial net transfer of resources to developing countries.

A Fifty-Year History of Development

The UN's development focus is no accident. The link between peace and development is embodied in the UN Charter itself. After the half-century of world war that led to the United Nations in 1945, both politicians and political theorists understood that an enduring peace could be built only upon a foundation of expanding prosperity and social justice. In this spirit, the Charter undertook "to employ international machinery for the promotion of economic and social advancement of all peoples. . . ."

Over the next 50 years, while the Security Council's deadlocks on "high political" issues got banner headlines during the Cold War, another United Nations emerged and flourished—a United Nations heavily engaged in operational activities with refugees and the internally displaced, with the poor and hungry, with child survival, with population and environmental initiatives, and with programs to promote democratic and human rights.

Indeed, the resources of the UN's program are heavily skewed towards those countries most in need and toward the most disadvantaged groups in societies, perhaps more so than any other development assistance entity. For millions in poor countries, these concrete programs of assistance *are* the United Nations.

The United Nations is not merely an international forum but the bearer of tangible benefits. The blue flag has the respect it does because it is the symbol of people helping other people build a just and sustainable world. Indeed, the United Nations has a track record second to none in promoting sustainable, equitable development. So, the most basic reason for strengthening the UN's development work is to build on success. Indeed, the UN's various funds and programs are the best things about the United Nations.

Six UN "Core Competencies"

Let me also enumerate the special strengths—the "comparative advantages" and "core competencies"—which the United Nations brings to the development table. There are six on my list:

(1) The United Nations provides a unique forum for raising public consciousness, defining the international development agenda and building the consensus needed for action. Once forged, consensus is translated into international norms and agreements, integrated into national development priorities, and supported through the UN's operational activities. Only the United Nations can provide leadership over this span.

(2) The neutrality of the United Nations means that it does not represent any particular national or commercial interest, or interests or "donors" generally. The United Nations can therefore develop special relationships of trust with countries and their people and can provide stable, long-term capacity-building assistance free of short-term political or economic objectives. This is very important, because trust facilitates some things essential to successful development cooperation, including candid policy dialogue, cooperation on sensitive matters such as political and economic transitions, and capacity-building for better and more open and transparent governance.

(3) The UN's universal presence means that it has the largest network of country offices and does not overlook any country. Moreover, the UN's extensive "field presence" is not superficial; its country offices are not liaison offices but major centers. The United Nations thus has a unique delivery capability, as well as unique capability to promote South-South cooperation.

198

(4) The United Nations emphasizes bottom-up, country-driven programming of development assistance resources, without conditionalities. These facts, plus developing country participation in UN's governance, ensures ownership of UN's development initiatives by the parties involved. Developing country ownership, in turn, is essential to sustainability and success.

The Challenges of the Future

Just as the nineteenth-century mechanisms of national government were inadequate for the challenges of the postwar era, so today's institution of international governance are inadequate for the challenges of the 21st century. Many of the basic elements of national governance will be needed in a more robust structure of global governance. An essential aspect of global governance, as of national governance, is responsibility to people—to equity, to justice, to enlarging the choices of all.

Some of the key institutions of global governance needed for the 21st century include:

• A stronger and more coherent United Nations to provide a forum for global leadership with equity and human concerns.

• A global central bank and lender of last resort.

• A World Trade Organization that ensures both free and fair international trade, with a mandate extending to global competition policy with antitrust provisions and a code of conduct for multinational corporations.

• A world environment agency.

• A world investment trust with redistributive functions.

• An international criminal court with a broader mandate for human rights.

• A broader UN system, including a two-chamber General Assembly to allow for civil society representation.

United Nations Development Programme, *Human Development Report 1999*.

(5) The UN's programs focus heavily on the neediest countries, on the neediest people within those countries, and on those countries where building effective governance is critical. The United Nations has special strengths and expe-

rience in the social, human and governance aspects of development, both with governments themselves and with civil society. If we use it properly, the United Nations has an important capability to promote participation in governance. (6) The United Nations has a comprehensive mandate, spanning social, economic and political issues. It can thus support political and economic transitions linked to development such as processes of democratization and market development. The United Nations has a capability to mobilize, deliver and coordinate humanitarian assistance and to promote reconstruction and reintegration in post-emergency situations. It can link work in peace-building refugees and relief, reconstruction and development, and it provides an ideal base for support for early warning and preventive development initiatives. This breadth is unique.

No other development assistance institution can point to such an array of assets and capabilities.

The Peace and Development Link

We know we want a United Nations that can promote peace, but if we want a UN for peace, we need a United Nations for development. Many critics of international assistance have not paused to think about the underlying causes of the conflicts in which the United Nations and others are becoming involved. Degrading poverty, diminishing natural resources, and increasing joblessness all feed ethnic and social tensions. It is from this cauldron that crises can boil over.

What a dramatic change we have witnessed in world affairs in recent decades, and how little we have understood it. Of 82 conflicts [since 1993]—each costing more than a thousand lives—79 have been *within* nations, not between nations. Ninety percent of the casualties are civilians, not combatants. These conflicts require development upstream, not soldiers downstream.

The UN should be strengthened as a bulwark for preventive initiatives around the globe. It should be made into a stronger human development agency, so that there are fewer internal conflicts and less need for relief and peacekeeping operations.

"In responding to human catastrophes, the U.N. consistently proves less resourceful, less honest and less brave than private aid organizations."

Humanitarian Efforts by the United Nations Are Ineffective

Peter Beinart

In the following viewpoint, Peter Beinart asserts that United Nations' attempts at providing aid to Third World nations are ineffective and create further problems. According to Beinart, the U.N. is too slow to act in famine-stricken and war-torn nations, and its delay results in numerous lost lives. Beinart also contends that the organization fails to confront the murderous governments that control many developing nations, particularly in Africa. He maintains that non-governmental organizations, including the Red Cross, are better able to provide food aid in Ethiopia and Somalia. Beinart is an editor at the *New Republic*.

As you read, consider the following questions:

1. In Beinart's opinion, why do Third World leaders praise the U.N.?
2. How many Somalians did the Red Cross feed in 1991 and 1992, according to the author?
3. What does Beinart believe is the chief failing of U.N. aid agencies?

D iscouraged by the U.N.'s irrelevance to the great military and political contests of its time, globalists often resort to a backup line of defense. Since the U.N. is not sovereign and lacks the ability to tax and conscript, they say, it cannot act as a world policeman. But that's okay because its true value lies in the less glamorous sphere of "low politics," where it manifests global conscience by delivering humanitarian relief to desperate populations: the U.N. as world social worker. The argument is morally resonant, especially when made by the Third World governments whose populations the U.N. succors. Unfortunately, however, in responding to human catastrophes, the U.N. consistently proves less resourceful, less honest and less brave than private aid organizations and national relief agencies. And this, of course, is precisely why it wins praise from those Third World leaders responsible for such catastrophes, leaders whose hold on power depends precisely on foreign humanitarians being neither resourceful nor honest, nor brave. A few examples.

Responses to the Ethiopian Famine

Ethiopia. Although Addis Ababa hosted one of the largest concentrations of permanent U.N. staff in Africa, the U.N. reacted slowly to the famine building in the Ethiopian countryside in the early 1980s. By 1982, nongovernmental organizations (NGOs) such as World Vision Relief and Catholic Relief Services were sounding alarm bells—redirecting their own resources to Ethiopia and asking the U.S. government for more. By contrast, the U.N. Disaster Relief Organization and the U.N. International Children's Fund did not launch appeals until the spring of 1983, and bureaucratic infighting between key U.N. agencies such as the World Food Program and the Food and Agricultural Organization kept them from publishing a report on the situation until June 1984. Even then, the report gravely underestimated the extent of the crisis. In his book *Reluctant Aid or Aiding the Reluctant*, Steven Varnis estimates that the U.N. did not fully mobilize until November 1984, thereby missing the chance to stem the hunger before it reached epidemic proportions.

But the real problem was less the U.N.'s failure to mobilize quickly than the nature of the mobilization itself. The

Ethiopian government of Mengistu Haile Mariam faced a rebellion in the northern province of Tigray. But Mengistu denied both that his regime had lost control of the province and that its inhabitants faced starvation. As a result, the government distributed less than 6 percent of its aid to a province that included one-third of those at risk from starvation.

Confronted with a host government unable and unwilling to grant them access to hundreds of thousands of its starving citizens, or even to acknowledge their existence, NGOs improvised. Norwegian Church Aid and other Protestant relief organizations, funded by the United States Agency for International Development (USAID), secretly funneled food from the Sudan into rebel-held areas in the Ethiopian north. The effort was bold and ingenious. Never before had aid groups transported such large stores of food across a border without the knowledge of the host government. The rebel-led welfare networks, which the NGOs assisted, constituted, in the words of the watchdog group African Rights, "the most effective relief programs ever mounted in a political emergency in Africa."

The U.N.'s response could not have been more different. Its Emergency Office for Ethiopia not only made no effort to reach the starving in rebel-held areas, it also legitimized Mengistu's claim that they did not exist. In August 1985, an Emergency Office report claimed that the government and the NGOs operating under its auspices were reaching 75 percent of the needy in Tigray. The actual figure was less than 15 percent. The office ignored repeated findings from journalists and independent monitors that as much as one-half to two-thirds of the food it gave the government for Tigray and the neighboring province of Eritrea was being diverted to the military. Says Alex de Waal, former co-director of Human Rights Watch-Africa: "It was criminal. . . . The U.N.'s role in that [cover-up] cost many lives and strengthened Mengistu. The government would have fallen years earlier without their help."

The Red Cross Is More Effective

Somalia. In January 1991, when dictator Mohammed Siad Barré fled Mogadishu, leaving chaotic inter-clan warfare in his wake, the U.N. fled as well. For almost all of 1991, as the situation deteriorated and anarchy turned to mass starvation, the U.N. stayed away. Meanwhile five private relief agencies, including the International Committee of the Red Cross, remained in Mogadishu. In December, Pierre Glassmann, the African Delegate-General for the Red Cross, demanded to know, "How come UNICEF-Somalia has thirteen people in Nairobi and no one in Somalia?" Marco Barsotti of the United Nations Development Program responded astoundingly, "In a situation of war, we don't operate."

A Mismanaged Organization

On non-military matters the UN's performance has been dreadful. The organization is plagued by problems of mismanagement and corruption. Much of the UN's energy and funds has been devoted to pushing such pernicious measures as the Law of the Sea Treaty and holding pretentious summits on the environment, world population, and other issues. Delegates to those gatherings habitually embrace the discredited notion that more government intervention and regulation are the solution to any problem.

Ted Galen Carpenter, *Cato Daily Commentaries*, November 18, 1997.

NGOs, particularly the Red Cross, stepped into the breach. Rather than wasting time developing new relief strategies, the Red Cross built upon local knowledge, essentially merging with the indigenous Somali Red Crescent Society. When a Somali woman, Dhababo Isse, found that cooked food was less often stolen by local militias because it could not be easily sold, the Red Cross used her soup kitchens as its national model. And rather than letting food pile up in warehouses in Mogadishu and Kismayo, where it was subject to the whim of local warlords, the Red Cross spread its deliveries across every port, and even some beaches, in southern Somalia.

Even when the U.N. began operations, almost a year later, they quickly became a fiasco. The U.N.'s World Food Program let large stores of food sit in the Mogadishu port while it worked out a complex distribution system, only to find them repeatedly looted. The U.N. Development Program left $68 million of its Somalia budget unspent for nine crucial months during 1992 because it lacked the signature of a nonexistent Somali official. United Nations High Commissioner for Refugees (UNHCR) and the World Food Program bickered for three months over a contract to distribute food by truck to a Somali refugee camp in the Hararghe region of Ethiopia, while in the camp fifty refugees died per day. The contrast with the Red Cross—which in 1991 and 1992 fed roughly 1.5 million people, more than all the U.N. agencies combined—could not be sharper.

The Future of Rwanda

Rwanda. In Rwanda, the U.N. is not leaving people to starve as it did in Ethiopia and Somalia. Yet its policies there may be sowing the seeds of future humanitarian disaster even as they prevent one today. Stung by its peacekeepers' hasty exit in the midst of one of the century's worst genocides, the U.N. [in 1994] moved quickly to provide for the mass of Hutu refugees streaming out of Rwanda ahead of the Tutsi-dominated Rwandan Patriotic Front. Yet even as the U.N. helped care for hundreds of thousands of Rwandan refugees, chronic interagency infighting and a myopic determination to remain "apolitical" stymied any attempt to identify and bring to justice those who had been responsible for the slaughter. One year later, the result is that former government militias, often armed and sometimes in uniform, control many U.N. refugee camps, terrorizing civilians and plotting to reinvade.

To be sure, private aid groups face the same excruciating dilemma of whether to deny food and medicine to hungry suspected murderers. But U.N. agencies have been the least willing to take steps to separate the ring-leaders from those on whom they prey. Christine Umutoni, Deputy Minister for Rehabilitation and Reintegration in Rwanda's new government, berates the U.N. for being "unwilling to take the steps necessary, through a special police force, to keep the killers away from the refugees." Janet Fleischmann of Human Rights Watch-Africa notes, "The U.N. clearly took the lead in assisting these refugees who were in uniform and armed . . . and that helped them establish control over the refugee camps." In protest, *Médecins sans Frontières* [Doctors Without Borders], along with several other NGOs, has begun pulling out of militia-controlled refugee camps in Zaire.

Meanwhile, the U.N. has spent less than half as much money on humanitarian and development efforts in devastated Rwanda itself as it has in the refugee camps. In July [1995], Richard McCall, USAID chief of staff, accused the U.N. of "doing a miserable job" of helping the new government. While U.N. officials complain that Western donors have not given them adequate resources, dumping more money into militia-controlled refugee camps might only hasten the day when the perpetrators of Rwanda's 1994 genocide reclaim their country.

The chief failing of the U.N. aid agencies is not that they are clumsy and lethargic but that they are dishonest. To maintain the support of the continent's leaders, they cling to the fiction that Africans suffer not from murderous government but from murderous weather. And since humans are not responsible for Africa's ills, they can pretend that humanitarian work need not require political and moral confrontation. The U.N. should have abandoned this conceit a decade ago, after its experience in Ethiopia. Because it did not, Rwanda's current peace may prove little more than a lull between killing seasons.

Periodical Bibliography

The following articles have been selected to supplement the diverse views presented in this chapter. Addresses are provided for periodicals not indexed in the *Readers' Guide to Periodical Literature*, the *Alternative Press Index*, the *Social Sciences Index*, or the *Index to Legal Periodicals and Books*.

J. Brian Atwood	"Midwife to Democracy: The Not-So-Ugly American," *New Perspectives Quarterly*, Fall 1996.
Salih Booker	"Thinking Regionally About Africa," *Current History*, May 1998.
Joel E. Cohen	"Why Should More United States Tax Money Be Used to Pay for Development Assistance in Poor Countries?" *Population and Development Review*, September 1997.
Chester A. Crocker	"Time to Get Serious in Africa," *New York Times*, August 28, 1998.
Seth Dunn	"Can the North and South Get in Step?" *World Watch*, November/December 1998.
Jane H. Ingraham	"Africa Enchained," *New American*, August 17, 1998. Available from American Opinion Publishing, 770 Westhill Blvd., Appleton, WI 54914.
Jesse Jackson	"Good Neighbors," *Liberal Opinion*, March 22, 1999. Available from PO Box 880, Vinton, IA 52349-0880.
R.W. Johnson	"U.S. Aid Undermines South Africa's Democracy," *Wall Street Journal*, September 21, 1998.
Robert D. Kaplan	"Proportionalism," *Atlantic Monthly*, August 1996.
Paul Lewis	"Downside of Doing Good: Disaster Relief Can Harm," *New York Times*, February 27, 1999.
Dave Peterson	"Finding African Solutions to African Problems," *Washington Quarterly*, Summer 1998.
Kenneth Roth	"American Failures in Africa," *Tikkun*, July/August 1998.
Frank Smyth	"A New Game: The Clinton Administration on Africa," *World Policy Journal*, Summer 1998.
I. William Zartman	"An Apology Needs a Pledge," *New York Times*, April 2, 1998.

For Further Discussion

Chapter 1

1. The first four viewpoints in this chapter debate production and consumption in Third World nations and whether Western lifestyles and economic policies would help or hinder developing populations. With whose argument(s) do you most agree? Explain your answer.

2. Helen Searls contends that Western feminists do not understand the concerns of Third World women. Do you agree with her view that Western values and attitudes toward women's issues should not be forced on developing nations? Why or why not?

3. Keith B. Richburg maintains that AIDS is spread in Africa by prostitution and polygamy. Charles L. Geshekter uses a variety of statistics to counter this argument. Which hypothesis do you think is more convincing? Explain your answer, drawing from the viewpoints and any other relevant material.

Chapter 2

1. According to Tim Carrington and Bryan T. Johnson, countries with limited economic freedom are less likely to develop. Do you agree with their conclusion that only nations with significant economic freedom can become fully developed? Why or why not?

2. Cardinal Roger Mahony and Martin Vander Weyer disagree on whether Third World debt should be reduced or cancelled. Whose argument do you agree with and why? If you think that debt reduction or cancellation is necessary, provide what you think would be a practical approach.

3. After reading the viewpoints by the World Bank and Bryan T. Johnson, do you think the World Bank has succeeded at its development goals? Explain your answer.

Chapter 3

1. James L. Tyson contends that the Anglo-American form of democracy will not succeed in a heterogeneous nation. Do you agree with his analysis or do you think that developing nations should model themselves after the United States? Explain your answer.

2. Amii Omara-Otunnu contends that South Africa's 1999 presidential election was successful because it had little violence and high turnout. *The Economist* argues that the election was prob-

lematic because it demonstrates how ruling parties become entrenched in Africa. Whose argument do you find more convincing and why?

3. The authors in this chapter examine the historical government and social structures of developing nations and consider how those structures might impact the future of Third World democracy. Based on the viewpoints and any other relevant readings, do you think that some developing nations might find it difficult to overcome a nondemocratic past? Explain your answer.

Chapter 4

1. J. Brian Atwood argues that Americans should support foreign aid programs because these programs will eventually benefit the U.S. economy. L. Jacobo Rodriguez asserts that the United States does not benefit from assistance programs because most recipients of foreign aid do not vote similarly to the United States when issues are debated at the United Nations. Should the U.S. political agenda be relevant in the foreign aid debate, or should the focus be restricted to the developing nations themselves? Explain your answer.

2. Ileana Ros-Lehtinen and the *Revolutionary Worker* disagree over the impact of American intervention in Africa. Whose argument do you find more convincing and why?

3. After reading the viewpoints in this chapter, do you think that foreign aid programs help or harm Third World nations? Explain your answer. Which type of programs (i.e. food aid), if any, do you consider most beneficial and why?

Organizations to Contact

The editors have compiled the following list of organizations concerned with the issues debated in this book. The descriptions are derived from materials provided by the organizations. All have publications or information available for interested readers. The list was compiled on the date of publication of the present volume; the information provided here may change. Be aware that many organizations take several weeks or longer to respond to inquiries, so allow as much time as possible.

Africa Faith and Justice Network (AFJN)
3035 Fourth St. NE, Washington, DC 20017
(202) 832-3412 • fax: (202) 832-9051
e-mail: afjn@afjn.org • website: http://www.acad.cua.edu/afjn
AFJN strives to be a meaningful voice for Africa in U.S. public policy. AFJN stresses issues of human rights and social justice that tie directly into Catholic social teaching. AFJN works closely with Catholic missionary congregations and numerous Africa-focused coalitions of all persuasions to advocate for U.S. economic and political policies that will benefit Africa's poor majority, facilitate an end to armed conflict, and establish development. AFJN publishes the monthly newsletter *Around Africa*.

Association for Women in Development (AWID)
666 11th St. NW, Suite 450, Washington, DC 20001
(202) 628-0440 • fax: (202) 628-0442
e-mail: awid@awid.org • website: http://www.awid.org
AWID is an international membership organization committed to gender equality and a just and sustainable development process. AWID facilitates a three-way exchange among scholars, practitioners, and policymakers in order to develop effective and transformative approaches for improving the lives of women and girls worldwide. AWID publishes *AWIDNews*, a quarterly newsletter that keeps members in touch with changes at AWID and in the *Global Women's Movement*. It includes reports on recent events, thought pieces on critical issues, career opportunities, resources, upcoming events, and advocacy updates.

Association of Third World Studies, Inc. (ATWS)
Center for International Studies, PO Box 8106
Georgia Southern University, Statesboro, GA 30460
(912) 681-0548 • fax: (912) 681-0824
e-mail: hisaacs@canes.gsw.edu • hisaacs@americus.net
website: http://www.wiu.edu/users/mfmbk/atws/
ATWS is the largest professional organization of its kind in the
world. With a global membership and chapters in South Asia and
Africa, members include academics, practitioners in the area of
Third World development, employees of government agencies,
and diplomats. The association holds international conferences
and publishes the *Journal of Third World Studies (JTWS)*, *ATWS
Conference Proceedings*, *ATWS Newsletter*, and the *ATWS Area Interest List*. In 1995 the United Nations granted ATWS "consulta-
tive status," enabling the association to increase its direct impact
on Third World issues and developments.

CARE
151 Ellis St. NE, Atlanta, GA 30303-2439
(800) 521-2273 ext. 999
e-mail: info@care.org • website: http://www.care.org
CARE is one of the world's largest international relief and development organizations. CARE helped train the first Peace Corps
volunteers in Latin America and became a leader in self-help development and food aid. CARE reaches over 35 million people in
over sixty developing and emerging nations in Africa, Asia, Latin
America, and Europe. CARE works to provide basic education for
children, economic and social empowerment for women, a stable
supply of food and clean water, basic health care, universal immu-
nization of children, and access to family planning services.
CARE publishes two quarterly reports, *World Report* and *Program
in Touch*, and an annual report.

Harvard Institute for International Development (HIID)
14 Story St., Cambridge, MA 02138
(617) 495-2161 • fax: (617) 495-0527
e-mail: info@hiid.harvard.edu
website: http://www.hiid.harvard.edu
HIID brings together the diverse resources of Harvard University
to assist developing and transitional nations in crafting polices to
accelerate their economic growth and improve the welfare of
their people. HIID publishes the series Harvard Studies in International Development, which discusses a variety of research activ-

ities conducted by HIID professional staff; a series of over seven hundred working papers called the Development Discussion Papers, which give early exposure to the work of the staff before it is published; and many other publications.

International Monetary Fund (IMF)
700 19th St. NW, Washington, DC 20431
(202) 623-7430 • fax: (202) 623-6278
website: http://www.imf.org

IMF's purpose is to promote international economic cooperation, to help keep a balance of trade among nations so that all benefit from the expansion of trade, and to lend its member nations money when necessary. It acts as a depository of information and statistical data regarding the economic affairs of its members. The fund publishes pamphlets, brochures, fact sheets, the semi-monthly *IMF Survey*, and an annual report.

North American Congress on Latin America (NACLA)
475 Riverside Dr., Suite 454, New York, NY 10115
(212) 870-3146 • fax: (212) 870-3305
e-mail: nacla@nacla.org • website: http://www.nacla.org

NACLA is an independent, nonprofit organization that provides policymakers, analysts, academics, organizers, journalists, and religious and community groups with information on major trends in Latin America and its relations with the United States. The core of NACLA's work is its bimonthly magazine *NACLA Report on the Americas*, the most widely read English language publication on Latin America.

North-South Institute (NSI)
55 Murray St., Suite 200, Ottawa, ON, K1N 5M3 Canada
(613) 241-3535 • fax: (613) 241-7435
e-mail: nsi@nsi-ins.ca • website: http://www.nsi-ins.ca/info.html

NSI is the only independent, nongovernmental research institute in Canada focused on international development. The institute's research supports global efforts to strengthen international development cooperation, improve governance in developing countries, enhance gender and social responsibility in globalizing markets, and prevent ethnic and other conflict. Its publications include books, briefing papers, special reports, speeches, an annual report, and a newsletter, *Review*. A catalogue of publications is available on NSI's homepage.

Population Council
1 Dag Hammarskjold Plaza, Floor 9, New York, NY 10017-2220
(212) 339-0500
e-mail: pubinfo@popcouncil.org
website: http://www.popcouncil.org
The Population Council is an international, nonprofit institution that conducts research on biomedical, social science, and public health. Focusing on developing countries, the Population Council develops contraceptives and other products to improve reproductive health, improves family planning and reproductive health services, and studies the causes and consequences of population growth. The Population Council publishes the *Policy Research Division (PRD) Working Papers* and the periodicals *Population and Development Review* and *Studies in Family Planning.*

U.S. Agency for International Development (USAID)
Ronald Reagan Building, Washington, DC 20523-0016
(202) 712-4810 • fax: (202) 216-3524
website: http://www.info.usaid.gov
USAID is the U.S. government agency that implements America's foreign economic and humanitarian assistance programs and provides assistance to countries recovering from disaster, trying to escape poverty, and engaging in democratic reforms. USAID is an independent federal government agency that receives overall foreign policy guidance from the secretary of state. The public may look up and order USAID documents, reports, and publications by using the agency's online database of one hundred thousand USAID technical and program documents.

The World Bank
1818 H St. NW, Washington, DC 20433
(202) 477-1234
website: http://www.worldbank.org
The World Bank is the world's largest source of development assistance, providing nearly $30 billion in loans annually to its client countries. The bank uses its financial resources and its extensive knowledge base to help each developing country onto a path of stable, sustainable, and equitable growth. The bank publishes many books and reports on the economies of the Third World, including *Accelerating China's Rural Transformation.*

Bibliography of Books

Haleh Afshar, ed.	*Women and Politics in the Third World.* London: Routledge, 1996.
George Akeya Agbango, ed.	*Issues and Trends in Contemporary African Politics: Stability, Development, and Democratization.* New York: Peter Lang, 1997.
Iftikhar Ahmed and Jacobus A. Doeleman, eds.	*Beyond Rio: The Environmental Crisis and Sustainable Livelihoods in the Third World.* New York: St. Martin's Press, 1995.
Claude Ake	*Democracy and Development in Africa.* Washington, DC: The Brookings Institution, 1996.
Chris Alden	*Apartheid's Last Stand: The Rise and Fall of the South African Security State.* London: Macmillan, 1996.
George B.N. Ayittey	*Africa in Chaos.* New York: St. Martin's Press, 1998.
Edward Bever	*Africa.* Phoenix, AZ: Oryx Press, 1996.
Roderic Ai Camp, ed.	*Democracy in Latin America: Patterns and Cycles.* Wilmington, DE: Scholarly Resources, 1996.
Robert Chase, Emily Hill, and Paul Kennedy, eds.	*The Pivotal States: A New Framework for U.S. Policy in the Developing World.* New York: W.W. Norton, 1999.
Earl Conteh-Morgan	*Democratization in Africa: The Theory and Dynamics of Political Transitions.* Westport, CT: Praeger, 1997.
Nikki Craske	*Women and Politics in Latin America.* New Brunswick, NJ: Rutgers University Press, 1999.
Larry Diamond and Marc F. Plattner, eds.	*Democracy in East Asia.* Baltimore, MD: Johns Hopkins University Press, 1998.
Robert N. Gwynne and Cristobal Kay, eds.	*Latin America Transformed: Globalization and Modernity.* Victoria, Australia: Edward Arnold, 1999.
Howard Handelman	*The Challenge of Third World Development.* Upper Saddle River, NJ: Prentice Hall, 1996.
Lawrence E. Harrison	*The Pan-American Dream: Do Latin America's Cultural Values Discourage True Partnership with the United States and Canada?* New York: BasicBooks, 1997.
Jeffrey Haynes	*Democracy and Civil Society in the Third World: Politics and New Political Movements.* Malden, MA: Polity Press, 1998.

Richard S. Hillman, ed.
Understanding Contemporary Latin America. Boulder, CO: Lynne Rienner, 1997.

Anil Hira
Ideas and Economic Policy in Latin America. Westport, CT: Praeger, 1998.

Thomas F. Homer-Dixon and Jessica Blitt, eds.
Ecoviolence: Links Among Environment, Population, and Security. Lanham, MD: Rowman & Littlefield, 1998.

Akio Hosono and Neantro Saavedra-Rivano, eds.
Development Strategies in East Asia and Latin America. New York: St. Martin's Press, 1998.

Robert D. Kaplan
The Ends of the Earth: A Journey at the Dawn of the 21st Century. New York: Random House, 1996.

Ray Kiely and Phil Marfleet, eds.
Globalisation and the Third World. London: Routledge, 1998.

Robin Luckham and Gordon White, eds.
Democratization in the South: The Jagged Wave. Manchester, United Kingdom: Manchester University Press, 1996.

Peter Marber
From Third World to World Class: The Future of Emerging Markets in the Global Economy. Reading, MA: Perseus Books, 1998.

Michael Maren
The Road to Hell: The Ravaging Effects of Foreign Aid and International Charity. New York: Free Press, 1997.

Michael Mason
Development and Disorder: A History of the Third World Since 1945. Hanover, NH: University Press of New England, 1997.

Marian A.L. Miller
The Third World in Global Environmental Politics. Boulder, CO: Lynne Rienner, 1995.

Heraldo Muñoz and Joseph S. Tulchin, eds.
Latin American Nations in World Politics. Boulder, CO: Westview Press, 1996.

Clark D. Neher and Ross Marlay
Democracy and Development in Southeast Asia: The Winds of Change. Boulder, CO: Westview Press, 1995.

Philip Oxhorn and Graciela Ducatenzeiler, eds.
What Kind of Democracy? What Kind of Market?: Latin America in the Age of Neoliberalism. University Park: Pennsylvania State University Press, 1998.

Philip Oxhorn and Pamela K. Starr, eds.
Markets & Democracy in Latin America: Conflict or Convergence? Boulder, CO: Lynne Rienner, 1998.

John Reader
Africa: A Biography of the Continent. New York: Knopf, 1998.

Keith B. Richburg
Out of America. New York: BasicBooks, 1997.

Mitchell A. Seligson and John T. Passe-Smith, eds. — *Development and Underdevelopment: The Political Economy of Global Inequality.* Boulder, CO: Lynne Rienner, 1998.

Harvey J. Sindima — *Africa's Agenda: The Legacy of Liberalism and Colonialism in the Crisis of African Values.* Westport, CT: Greenwood Press, 1995.

Brian C. Smith — *Understanding Third World Politics: Theories of Political Change and Development.* Bloomington: Indiana University Press, 1996.

Donald M. Snow — *Distant Thunder: Patterns of Conflict in the Developing World.* Armonk, NY: M.E. Sharpe, 1997.

Allister Sparks — *Tomorrow Is Another Country: The Inside Story of South Africa's Road to Change.* New York: Hill and Wang, 1995.

Eugene Versluysen — *Defying the Odds: Banking for the Poor.* West Hartford, CT: Kumarian Press, 1999.

Georgina Waylen — *Gender in Third World Politics.* Boulder, CO: Lynne Rienner, 1996.

Index

Museveni, Yoweri, 137–38, 186
Mwangi, James, 141

Nakajima, Hiroshi, 70
natural resources
  are not critical for economic growth,
    26–27
  effect of population growth on, 22,
    23, 25
  and lifestyles, 38–40
Ndlovu, Martha, 48
New World Order, 128
Nicholson-Lord, David, 36
Nigeria, 137
  foreign investment in, is exploitive,
    186–87
  governments in, 135, 140
nongovernmental organizations (NGOs)
  and cultural practices, 204
  humanitarian aid of, is effective,
    202–205
  and women, 47, 51–54
  and World Bank, 109
Notestein, Frank, 40

Obasanjo, Olusegun, 135, 136, 140
O'Donnell, Guillermo, 157
Olson, Mancur, Jr., 177
Omara-Otunnu, Amii, 134
Ouattara, Alassane D., 79
Oxfam (relief organization), 53

peacekeeping missions, 160, 168
Perry, William, 165–66
Peru, 144
Peterson, Carl M., 191
Peterson, Dave, 194
Pinheiro, Paulo Sérgio, 151
political parties, 147–50
polygamy, 57, 58–60
Population Action International, 22
population growth
  causes economic problems, 22–23
    con, 24–29
  and consumption levels, 21–23
  cycles of, 20, 40
  and economic development, 20, 21
  effects of, on natural resources, 22,
    23, 25
  family planning is necessary, 23
  increases food production, 28
    con, 22
  projections of, 20, 37, 169
poverty
  command economies result in, 33–34
  foreign aid does not alleviate, 174
  and health care, 69–70
    AIDS, 60–61, 62

and international debt, 93–94, 96,
  101, 105, 110
is women's greatest problem, 41, 51,
  54–55
and violence, 153–57
pregnancy, 43, 51
Preston, Lewis T., 119
productivity
  restrictions on, are harmful, 31–35
  results from human activity, 26, 28
prostitution, 45
  and AIDS, 57–58, 61
Purvis, Andrew, 160

Rabushka, Alvin, 176
Red Cross, 204, 205, 206
Reed, Lawrence W., 33
refugees, 167–68
  from Rwanda, 180–81, 205–206
  from Somalia, 205
Regnery, Frederick, 30
religion
  and democracies, 129–30
Reluctant Aid or Aiding the Reluctant
  (Varnis), 202
reproductive tract infections, 44–45
Revolutionary Worker (newspaper), 184
Richburg, Keith B., 56
Robinson, Randall, 186
Rodriguez, L. Jacobo, 170
Ros-Lehtinen, Ileana, 179
Ruhl, J. Mark, 148
Rwanda
  government of, 137–38
  humanitarian aid in, 205–206
  refugees from, 180–81
  and United Nations, 205–206

Sachs, Ignacy, 154
Sachs, Jeffrey, 101
Science (magazine), 20
Searls, Helen, 50
sex
  in Africa
    attitudes toward, cause AIDS, 57–60
      con, 65, 66–67
    prevalence of, 65–66
sexually transmitted diseases, 44–45,
  47, 57–58
Shalikashvili, John, 165–66
Simons, Anna, 160
Singapore, 29
Solomon, Lawrence, 73
Somalia
  cultural practices and government of,
    191–92, 194
  humanitarian aid in, 203–205
  military intervention in, 160, 189

and United Nations, 203–205
South Africa
  cultural practices and government of,
    194–95
  governments in, 135–37, 140
  U.S. policy toward, 188–89
South Korea, 175
Speth, James Gustave, 196
State in a Changing World, The (World
  Development Report), 81, 82
Stein, Dorothy, 39
sustainable development concept, 118

Taiwan, 175
Tanzania, 141
Tobin Tax, 89
Toler, Deborah, 17–18
trade, 32
trade unions, 147–48
transnational corporations (TNCs). *See*
  multinational corporations
Tyson, James L., 126

Uganda
  AIDS in, 69
  economic development in, 80
  free-market economy of, 186
  government of, 137–38
  political parties in, 142
Umutoni, Christine, 205
unemployment, 28–29
United Nations
  Conference on Trade and
    Development (UNCTAD), 85, 87
  and development assistance
    core competencies of, 198–200
    is successful, 197–98
    should be strengthened, 200
  Fourth World Conference on
    Women (Beijing), 50–51, 53–55
  and global governance, 199
  and humanitarian aid
    is ineffective, 202–206
    is mismanaged, 204, 206
  maintain dictatorships, 202–203
  and multinational corporations, 89
  New International Economic Order,
    86
  Population Fund (UNFPA), 40–41
United States
  Agency for International Development
    (USAID), 162, 163, 178
  budget of, 164–65
  and nongovernmental
    organizations, 203
  Defense Intelligence Agency, 166–67
  policy toward Africa
    is imperialistic, 185–89

lacks coherence, 180–83
USA Today, 165–66

Vander Weyer, Martin, 100
Varnis, Steven, 202
venereal diseases. *See* sexually
  transmitted diseases
Venezuela, 145
violence
  gender-based, 45–46, 52, 53–54
  and government policies, 152–53,
    156–57
  and poverty, 153–57

Wacieni, Kaniaru, 141
Wolfensohn, James D., 112
Womankind Worldwide, 52, 53
women
  and AIDS, 44, 57
  Beijing conference on, 50–51, 53–55
  circumcision of, 46–47, 67
  and cultural practices, 46–48, 53–54,
    67
  feminist agenda is wrong focus,
    51–55
  health of, 43–47, 49
    and sexual freedom, 47–49
  and nongovernmental organizations,
    47, 51–54
  poverty of, is greatest problem, 41,
    51, 54–55
  violence against, 45–46, 52, 53–54
World Bank
  and HIPC, 96, 98, 104, 110
  and international debt, 95, 96
  and International Development
    Agency (IDA), 110, 118
  and International Finance
    Corporation, 77
  and International Monetary Fund, 109
  is effective, 107–15, 119
    con, 119–22
  and nongovernmental organizations,
    109
  policies of, must be changed, 17–18,
    112–13
  purpose of
    currently, 108, 113, 118–19
    originally, 117–18
World Federation of Trade Unions
  (WFTU), 84, 87, 88, 89
World Health Organization, 66, 68
World Trade Organization, 199

Yunis, Muhammad, 73

Zaire, 180–81
  see also Congo

221